Why bother with roller coasters when you can revel in the nail-biting thrill of watching paint dry? It's like an Olympic sport for your couch, and let's be honest—finding a matching sock is just a bonus!

ChatGPT

and

Paul Lloyd Hemphill

Also by Paul Lloyd Hemphill
(with serious vibes)

BOOKS
Gettysburg Lessons In The Digital Age
Why You're Already A Leader
Inspiration For Teens
Inspiration For Skeptics
Max Your Leadership!
You're Awesome!
Planning For College
How To Play The College Game

VIDEOS
America's 52 Stories

Dedicated to the humor-deprived and those who still think "knock-knock" jokes are cutting-edge comedy.

This non-fiction nutty book is available for educational, business, or promotional use! Really? Who knew learning could be this hilarious? For more information, contact the author at the website of American Education Defenders Dot Org where we promise not to send you unsolicited cat memes!

Watching Paint Dry

Cover Design by Waqas

Library of Congress Control Number: 2024922985
ISBN: 9798227882677

1. Humor 2. Non-fiction 3. Teen Humor

INTRODUCTION

The Thrills of the Mundane: An AI-Generated Rollercoaster with Paul Lloyd Hemphill as Your Fearless Co-Pilot!

Welcome to a world where the ordinary becomes extraordinary, and even the simplest tasks transform into epic adventures—thanks to our robot overlords! That's right, folks; this collection of hilariously absurd tales was primarily crafted by AI, with Paul Lloyd Hemphill swooping in like a word-wrangling superhero to tweak a few phrases. Think of him as the sidekick who forgot his cape but brought plenty of snacks!

Have you ever found yourself staring at a toaster, willing it to pop your bread, as if it's some sort of caffeinated deity? Or perhaps you've wrestled with a tangle of headphones that seemed more determined than a cat on a mission to ruin your Zoom call? Fear not! You are not alone in this epic saga of the everyday.

In these 55 delightfully ridiculous stories, we tackle the pulse-pounding suspense of waiting for water to boil and the heart-stopping thrill of replacing a lightbulb—hold onto your seats, folks! Who knew that folding laundry could feel like an Olympic sport where the gold medal is just a pair of clean socks?

Each tale is a testament to our uncanny ability to transform the mundane into the magnificent and the boring into belly-aching hilarity.

So grab a snack (preferably one that doesn't require an hour in the microwave) and settle in as we embark on this laugh-out-loud journey through life's most laughable moments. From the "excitement" of watching paint dry to the nail-biting experience of filling out tax forms, we promise to tickle your funny bone and remind you just how absurd our daily routines can be.

Get ready to laugh until you snort, roll your eyes at the sheer ridiculousness, and nod in agreement as we explore the wild side of chores—because sometimes, the most thrilling adventures are hiding in the least thrilling places! Enjoy the ride—AI wrote it, and Paul just tried not to break it

ChatGPTI (and Paul Lloyd Hemphill who's enjoying the snacks)

Table of Contents - Forget page numbers - just follow the story numbers and let the flipping fun begin!

34. As Riveting as Watching Dust Settle
35. As Enchanting as Waiting for a Train that's Late
36. As Dramatic as Making Your Bed
37. As Thrilling as Buying Groceries
38. As Exciting as Waiting for the Wi-Fi to Reconnect
39. As Engaging as Watching Your Pet Sleep
40. As Gripping as Watching Laundry Spin in the Dryer
41. As Spellbinding as Reading the Ingredients on a Bag of Chips
42. As Intense as Picking the Right Toothpaste
43. As Action-Packed as Organizing Your Pens
44. As Gripping as Sorting Through Old Receipts
45. As Intriguing as Checking the Weather App for the 10th Time
46. As Entertaining as Waiting for Your Favorite Show to Buffer
47. As Dramatic as Cleaning Out the Refrigerator
48. As Riveting as Watching a Candle Burn
49. As Gripping as Preparing for a Conference Call
50. As Exciting as Watching the Mailman Arrive
51. As Engaging as Waiting for a Simmering Sauce
52. As Captivating as Listening to Elevator Music
53. As Mind-Numbing as Searching for a Lost Sock
54. As Absorbing as Staring at a Wall
55. As Electrifying as Reading the Directions on a Can of Soup
57. As Boring as Filling Out Forms
58. As Exciting as Watching Grass Grow
58. As Gripping as Watching a Snail Rac
59. As Captivating as Sorting Your Socks
60. As Exciting as Watching Your Phone Load a Video
61. As Exciting as Watching Your Hair Dry
62. As Boring as Watching Your Bread Toast
63. As Thrilling as Watching Water Boil
64. As Exciting as Watching Your Phone Charge
65. As Captivating as Watching Your Leaves Fall
66. As Exciting as Watching Your Pet Sleep
67. As Exciting as Watching Ice Cream Melt
68. As Engaging as Watching Your Friend Scroll on Their Phone
69. As Gripping as Watching Your Neighbor Mow Their Lawn
70. As Exciting as Watching Your Shoes Dry
71. As Compelling as Watching Your Dishwasher Run

1. As Fun as Counting Sheep

Lying in bed, Liam stared at the ceiling. The clock on his nightstand read 10:15 PM, but it felt like he'd been there for hours, sleep stubbornly refusing to come. With a groan, he rolled over and muttered, "Well, guess it's time to count sheep."

He closed his eyes and pictured a white fence. A single fluffy sheep trotted up to it, gave a half-hearted hop, and floated lazily over. "One sheep," he whispered.

A second sheep appeared, but this one seemed distracted, wandering around before finally leaping the fence, almost tripping on its own wool. "Two sheep," Liam muttered, sighing in frustration.

Then came sheep number three—except this one wasn't having it. It stood in front of the fence, staring Liam down like it had better things to do. "Go on!" he urged. The sheep responded by plopping down and taking a nap of its own.

Liam rubbed his eyes. "You've got to be kidding me."

Determined to make this work, Liam refocused. The fourth sheep approached the fence and then, out of nowhere, decided to moonwalk over it. "Okay, fine, that's cool, I guess," Liam muttered, shaking his head.

By the time the fifth sheep showed up, wearing sunglasses and casually flipping through a magazine, Liam had had enough. "What kind of sheep are these?!"

Now fully awake, Liam realized he'd entered some sort of bizarre dream-prevention program. The sixth sheep was in a full tuxedo, taking a bow before elegantly hopping over the fence.

"Seven sheep," he groaned, counting the next one—who was inexplicably wearing a jetpack.

Sheep eight burst onto the scene riding a unicycle. "This isn't helping!" Liam exclaimed, sitting up in bed.

By the time sheep nine paraglided over the fence, Liam was done. "I give up!" he shouted, throwing off his blanket. He stomped downstairs, deciding that a midnight snack might be more effective than these chaotic sheep.

Ironically, as soon as he opened the fridge, Liam yawned. He shuffled back to bed and finally drifted off—without counting another sheep.

2. As Fast-Paced as a Snail Race

It was a Saturday afternoon, and Finn, bored out of his mind, stared at his backyard, the epitome of dull. "Hey, why don't we have a snail race?" his sister Chloe suggested, pointing to the trail of snails inching their way across the damp ground.

"A snail race?" Finn raised an eyebrow. "That sounds about as fast-paced as... well, a snail race."

But with nothing better to do, they rounded up a few sluggish competitors, plopped them in a starting line of twigs, and waited. And waited.

"This is riveting," Finn deadpanned as the snails moved at a pace slower than his will to live. Chloe, determined to inject some excitement, grabbed a stick and crouched down next to her chosen snail. "C'mon, Turbo, you can do it! Look at that form!"

Finn smirked. "Turbo? That's like naming a glacier Speedy."

As the snails crept forward, Chloe got more invested. "Look at that! Turbo is pulling ahead!" she cheered, even though the difference in snail positions was barely noticeable. She grabbed a magnifying glass. "You've got this! Don't let Shelly catch up!"

Finn, not to be outdone, crouched next to his snail, Gary. "Listen, buddy, this is your moment. You've been training your whole life for this, all seven days of it. Show them what you've got."

The snails continued their sluggish crawl. After a full five minutes, Turbo was now half an inch ahead of Gary. Chloe, now on her feet, was in full sports commentator mode. "And Turbo's in the lead! But here comes Gary, closing the gap. This could be the upset of the century!"

Finn chuckled. "This might actually be the most boring thing I've ever done."

Another few minutes passed, and Chloe, in a final burst of enthusiasm, screamed, "It's neck and neck! Gary's—" She paused, squinting. "Wait... Gary's asleep?"

Finn sighed, poking the tiny shell. Gary wasn't just asleep—he was refusing to move entirely.

"Well, that's it. Turbo wins," Chloe said, doing a victory dance. Finn threw his hands up. "Who knew a snail race could be this exhilarating?"

As they packed up, Finn laughed. "Next time, let's race turtles. I want some real action."

3. As Thrilling as Waiting for Water to Boil

Mark stood by the stove, glaring at the pot of water. "This is taking forever," he groaned. His mom, calmly sipping tea, offered, "Why don't you do something while you wait?"

Mark wasn't convinced. "Like what? Watch it boil?"

With nothing better to do, he leaned in, staring at the pot as if sheer willpower could speed things up. "Come on, bubbles, do your thing."

Five minutes later, not a single bubble had appeared. Mark sighed dramatically. "I feel like I'm in a suspense movie, but nothing's happening!"

His mom chuckled. "Maybe you're using the wrong technique. Try a chant or something."

Mark raised an eyebrow. "Boil, boil, toil and trouble?" he muttered, waving his hands over the pot like a wizard. Still nothing.

Desperate, he started narrating. "The pot stood motionless. The tension in the air was thick as steam... only there was no steam. Would it ever boil?"

Finally, a single tiny bubble rose from the bottom of the pot. Mark gasped. “Oh my gosh! It’s happening!” He ran to the sink to grab pasta, only to return and find the bubble... had popped.

Mark threw his hands up. “This is worse than waiting for my birthday.”

Ten minutes later, when the water finally boiled, Mark threw the pasta in like it was the most epic moment of his life. "Victory!" he shouted.

4. As Adventurous as Folding Laundry

"Time for adventure!" Julie’s mom called from the living room. Julie sprinted in, her face lighting up with excitement—only to be met with a mountain of laundry.

Her mom grinned mischievously. "Today, we embark on the great Laundry Folding Quest!"

Julie looked at the pile, then back at her mom. "I thought this was going to be something cool. This is as adventurous as reading the dictionary."

But her mom wasn’t deterred. She handed Julie a mismatched sock. "Behold! The Lost Sock of Sockland! It’s been separated from its mate for centuries. Will you accept the quest to reunite them?"

Julie blinked. "Sure... I guess.”

As they folded, her mom invented a story. "The T-shirts are warriors, fighting to keep the kingdom of Laundryland safe. The towels are their mighty shields."

Julie rolled her eyes, but after a few minutes, she found herself getting into it. "Okay, but this sock? It's actually an undercover spy. I think it might be working for the evil Laundry Monster."

They spent the next half-hour folding socks and creating wild backstories for them. By the time the laundry was done, Julie had to admit it was slightly more fun than she'd expected. Slightly.

5. As Fast-Paced as Watching Ice Melt

Dan stared at the ice cube on the counter. "This... is so slow," he groaned, watching as the tiny cube seemed to refuse to melt.

"It's like the world's slowest action scene," his friend Greg said, sitting beside him. "Like a car chase in slow motion."

Dan smirked. "If this were a movie, we'd be on the edge of our seats, waiting for something dramatic to happen. Any second now..."

They both leaned in as a small drop of water formed at the bottom of the cube. "There it is!" Greg cheered. "We've got movement!"

Dan threw his hands up. "One drop in ten minutes? I could've read a novel by now."

As the cube shrank imperceptibly, the two friends started narrating the "action" like sportscasters. "And the ice cube is making its move! The tension is unbearable, folks! Will it melt completely before dinner? Only time will tell!"
Half an hour later, when the ice had finally turned into a small puddle, Greg stood up. "Well, that was exhausting. Next time, let's watch something faster. Like paint dry."

6. As Intense as a Game of Checkers with a Sloth

Oliver was pretty sure he had just entered the most intense match of his life—against a sloth.

The sloth, sitting across from him on a low branch, stared at the checkers board with a laser-like focus, though Oliver wasn't sure if that was just how sloths looked when they were confused.

"Your move," Oliver said, trying to encourage his opponent.

The sloth blinked. Slowly, painstakingly, it raised its arm. Oliver leaned in with anticipation The arm hovered over the board. It hung there. Oliver's excitement grew. Then... nothing.

"Is... is this your strategy?" Oliver asked. The sloth blinked again, then very, very slowly moved a single piece. After what felt like a century, the checker landed in its new spot.

Oliver threw up his hands. "Okay, great move. Now it's my turn." He quickly hopped his piece across the board, taking two of the sloth's checkers. "Boom! Double jump!"

The sloth didn't seem fazed. It blinked again, making eye contact as if to say, "Nice try, kid."

Thirty minutes later, they were still playing the same game. Oliver sighed. "I think I'm starting to age."

By the time the sloth finally made its second move, Oliver was ready to declare it the most intense game of his life. But maybe next time, he'd challenge something faster. Like a rock

7. As Captivating as Watching Clouds Drift

Sam lay on the grass, staring at the sky, where clouds drifted lazily across the blue expanse.

"Do you think we'll see something interesting?" his sister Emma asked.

"I mean... it's just clouds," Sam replied. "How interesting can it get?"

But Emma was determined. "Look! That one looks like a bunny!" she said, pointing excitedly.

Sam squinted. "More like a blob. A really puffy blob."

They continued staring, narrating the clouds as they passed. "There goes a dragon!" Emma exclaimed. Sam rolled his eyes. "That's a blob too. Just a big one."

For the next twenty minutes, they continued pointing out vaguely-shaped blobs in the sky, laughing at their ridiculous descriptions. "That one's definitely a marshmallow," Sam decided.

"Okay, but this one looks like... a turtle on a skateboard!" Emma said.

Sam glanced at her. "Are we even looking at the same sky?"

8. As Epic as a Postcard Collection

Mia shuffled through her shoebox full of postcards. "This is the most epic collection ever," she declared to her best friend, Alex, who sat beside her, trying to stifle a yawn.

"Epic? We're looking at pictures of places neither of us have been," Alex replied, raising an eyebrow.

"No, no, you don't get it," Mia said, waving one postcard in the air. "This one's from my cousin in Paris. See the Eiffel Tower? I mean, the romance, the glamour!"

Alex blinked. "I see a picture of a metal triangle."

Mia huffed. "Well, what about this one? From Rome! The Colosseum—imagine gladiators fighting right there. Can you feel the history?"

Alex squinted at the postcard. "I feel like I'm looking at an old postcard."

Mia wasn't about to give up. She dug through the box, pulling out another card triumphantly. "Ah, this is my favorite. It's from my grandma in Iowa. See? A cornfield. The landscape of dreams."

Alex snorted. "Epic. Truly. A field of corn."

Despite the lack of enthusiasm from her friend, Mia continued explaining the backstory behind every single postcard, as if each one were an ancient artifact from a distant land. By the time she got to her postcard from Delaware ("It's small but mighty!"), Alex was half-asleep.

"Yeah, maybe one day you'll get one from, I dunno, Antarctica. Then things will really spice up," Alex muttered, closing her eyes.

Mia's face lit up. "Now *that* would be epic. Penguins, glaciers, *the* South Pole—"

But Alex was already snoring

9. As Mysterious as a Puzzle with One Missing Piece

It was hour three of the jigsaw puzzle, and Nick was officially convinced that the missing piece was a government conspiracy.

"Where is it?" he muttered, scouring the table like a detective on the brink of cracking a major case. His sister Lily sat on the couch, watching him with an amused grin.

"I told you it's probably under the table," Lily said.

Nick ignored her. "This isn't just a puzzle. This is a mystery of the ages." He grabbed the puzzle box, shaking it. No piece. He looked under the couch cushions, behind the TV, even inside his shoes—nothing.

Lily yawned. "It's just a piece of sky. You can't even tell."

"Oh, I'll know. I'll know forever," Nick said, eyes wide, as if haunted by the puzzle gods.

For another fifteen minutes, Nick crawled on the floor, checking every nook and cranny in the room. "Maybe it fell into another dimension," he theorized, opening the fridge and glancing inside just in case the missing piece had a taste for leftovers.

Finally, he sat down, defeated. "I'm never doing a puzzle again."

Lily smirked, holding up the missing piece she'd been hiding the whole time. "Found it."

Nick stared at her, utterly baffled. "You've been holding that the whole time?!"

"Well, you were on a roll. Didn't want to ruin the mystery.

10. As Engaging as Rearranging the Pantry

It was a Saturday morning, and Jen had made the questionable decision to reorganize her pantry. "I'm going to put everything in alphabetical order!" she declared to her brother, Kyle, who was sitting at the kitchen counter munching on cereal.

"That sounds like the most boring thing ever," Kyle said between bites. "Like, 'Wow, can't wait to see where you'll put the quinoa.'"

But Jen was undeterred. She started pulling cans and boxes off the shelves. "Beans, beets, bread crumbs... it's going to be a masterpiece."

Kyle looked skeptical. "What's next, organizing the spices by height?"

Jen stopped mid-can-pull, her eyes lighting up. "That's actually a great idea! Short spices in front, tall in the back. I'm a pantry genius!"

For the next hour, Jen obsessively moved everything around, creating what she called "the ultimate pantry system." Kyle watched her place cans with surgeon-like precision, occasionally making sarcastic commentary.

"Wow, the mustard's next to the ketchup? Bold choice."

By the time she finished, the pantry looked like a grocery store display. "Ta-da!" she said, stepping back to admire her work.

Kyle, unimpressed, shrugged. "Cool. I give it two days before it's a mess again."

Jen smiled confidently. “Not this time. I’ve got a chart.” She pulled out a color-coded diagram of where everything belonged.

Kyle shook his head. “You’ve officially gone too far. Next, you’ll be alphabetizing the cereal boxes.”

Jen raised an eyebrow. “Hmm... that’s not a bad idea.”

11. As Fast as Filling Out Tax Forms

Ben sat down at the kitchen table, a stack of tax forms in front of him, and sighed. "This is going to be a breeze," he said with misplaced confidence.

His wife, Katie, peeked in from the living room. "Sure. Like filling out tax forms is ever a ‘breeze.’"

Ben waved her off. "No, no. I’ve got this. It’s just numbers, right?"

Twenty minutes later, Ben was staring at the forms as if they were written in an ancient language. "What’s a 1099 again?"

Katie smirked. "Oh, it’s only the thing you’ve been dealing with for the past five years."

Ben scratched his head. "And what’s this? Line 47B? How many lines can they *possibly* need?!"

Soon, the living room floor was covered in papers. Ben was muttering numbers to himself like some sort of tax wizard who had lost his spellbook.

Katie walked by, glancing at the chaos. "How’s that breeze going?"

"I’m in tax purgatory," Ben groaned. "This is slower than waiting for molasses to drip."

An hour later, Ben threw his hands up. "I give up. Maybe I’ll just declare my dog as a dependent and call it a day."

Katie patted him on the shoulder. "Or, you know, you could read the instructions."

"Instructions?" Ben asked, genuinely surprised. He glanced at the paper he'd ignored at the start. "Oh..."

Three hours and a lot of head-scratching later, Ben finally finished the forms. "See? Easy," he said triumphantly, even though he looked like he'd aged five years in the process.

Katie chuckled. "Next year, let's just hire an accountant."

12. As Surprising as an Empty Birthday Piñata

"Prepare for the ultimate piñata showdown!" yelled Evan, holding a broomstick in one hand while his friends gathered around, excitement buzzing in the air.

It was his 12th birthday, and the piñata—a rainbow-colored donkey—hung from the tree like a festive punching bag of joy. The kids lined up, ready for a candy explosion.

Evan took the first swing, blindfolded and determined. "Here comes the sugar rush!" he cried as he landed a solid hit on the piñata.

It didn't budge.

"Well, that's a tough one," said his friend Sam. "Let me have a go." Sam, with the focus of a piñata ninja, swung... and swung again... but the donkey just swayed in the breeze.

One by one, each kid took turns whacking the stubborn piñata. The tension grew. "This thing's invincible," complained Jake after his third try.

Finally, with a mighty swing, the piñata burst open—and the kids all screamed with excitement.

Only... nothing fell out.

The crowd gasped. “Where’s the candy?!”

Evan’s mom, laughing from the sidelines, approached. “Oops! I forgot to fill it! Sorry, kids!”

Evan stared at the empty piñata, utterly betrayed. “This is the biggest letdown of my life.”

13. As Electrifying as a Dead Phone Battery

Lucy stared at her phone screen, the dreaded “1% battery” warning flashing at her. "I’ve got time," she mumbled to herself, refusing to plug it in just yet.

Her friend Mike, sitting next to her on the couch, glanced over. “You know that thing’s about to die, right?”

“I’m living on the edge,” Lucy replied, scrolling through her social media as if she were in a race against time. Every second felt precious. Every swipe could be the last.

The minutes dragged on. She refreshed her feed again and again, like a gambler pulling the slot machine handle one last time, hoping for a miracle. Her phone screen dimmed to conserve power, the final warning that doom was near.

"You’re really risking it, huh?" Mike said with a smirk, holding his fully charged phone as if it were a trophy of responsible adulthood.

Lucy kept scrolling. “I’ve got this. Just one more meme—”

Her phone went black.

“Nooo!” Lucy groaned dramatically. “This is the worst feeling in the world!”

Mike raised an eyebrow. “Really? Worse than stepping on a Lego?”

Lucy sighed, tossing her phone onto the couch. “Okay, maybe not worse than Legos. But it’s up there.”

For the next hour, Lucy sat in battery-less silence, contemplating her poor life choices while Mike smugly played a game on his fully charged phone. “Plug it in next time,” he teased.

"Never," she muttered. “I’ll take my chances.”

14. As Riveting as Watching Bread Rise

Emily had decided to bake bread from scratch for the first time. Armed with flour, yeast, and an unreasonable amount of optimism, she mixed the dough and set it on the counter to rise.

“Now what?” she asked her brother, Dan, who had somehow been roped into this culinary adventure.

“Now we wait,” he said, settling into a kitchen chair like he was about to watch the most boring movie ever made.

Emily frowned. “How long does it take?”

Dan shrugged. “I don’t know. A couple hours?”

They both stared at the lump of dough, which sat on the counter, motionless.

“So... we just watch it?” Emily asked.

Dan smirked. “Yeah, it’s like the baking version of a nature documentary. And here we see the wild dough in its natural habitat...”

Emily laughed. “Shh! You’ll scare it. Dough can smell fear.”

The two of them sat there, pretending the dough was an exotic animal about to do something amazing, but it just... didn’t. The dough sat there like a lazy cat, not growing, not moving, not even twitching.

“I feel like I’ve aged five years,” Dan said after the first hour, slumped in his chair.

Finally, after what felt like an eternity, the dough puffed up, just slightly. Emily clapped. “It’s alive!”

Dan squinted at it. “I think it’s still dead inside. Much like me after watching bread rise.”

15. As Strategic as Untangling Christmas Lights

Elliot held up the tangled mass of Christmas lights like it was a snarled ball of yarn left behind by an angry cat. “This is going to take years,” he muttered.

His sister, Claire, watched from the couch. “Should’ve packed them better last year.”

“Should’ve,” Elliot agreed, but that wasn’t helping him now. He began gingerly pulling at a string of lights, trying to find the end. It was like navigating a maze, only the maze hated you and wanted to see you suffer.

"Careful," Claire warned, half-joking, "one wrong move and they’ll knot up even worse."

Elliot paused, his eyes narrowing. “This is like disarming a bomb.”

For the next twenty minutes, he worked meticulously, muttering under his breath. “If I could just… get this loop over that knot… we might survive.”

Claire had long since given up watching, now scrolling through her phone. “I told you, just buy new lights. Untangling those is a fool’s errand.”

“No way,” Elliot said, shaking his head. “This is personal now. The lights won’t defeat me.”

Finally, after what seemed like hours, he managed to free one end of the lights. “Aha! Victory!”

Claire glanced up, unimpressed. “Congrats. Now you just have 80 more feet of tangled wire to go.”

16. As Fast as Growing a Beard

Jason decided it was time. Time to grow a beard. He’d seen enough commercials for beard oils and waxes—he wanted that rugged, mountain-man look. He stared in the mirror, his chin as smooth as a baby’s cheek, and nodded to himself. "Today is the day."

Day one: nothing.

Day two: still nothing.

By day seven, he had a faint shadow, but it was the kind of shadow you had to squint to see. "I feel like I’m growing grass on my face," he muttered.

His friend, Ryan, smirked. “You sure you’re not just imagining it?”

“No, I’m serious! Look closely!” Jason pointed to his chin, where the “beard” had begun its slow march toward greatness.

Ryan leaned in. “Hmm. Maybe if you tilt your head in the right light, I can kind of see... something.”

Weeks went by, and the beard still wasn’t exactly giving off lumberjack vibes. But Jason was determined. “Greatness takes time,” he told himself in the mirror.

Ryan shook his head. “At this rate, you’ll be ready to chop wood... in 2028.”

17. As Exciting as a Dentist Waiting Room

Olivia sat in the dentist’s waiting room, flipping through a three-year-old magazine that might as well have been written in another era. "This is the highlight of my week," she said sarcastically.

Her friend Mia, who had come along for moral support, looked around at the bland posters of tooth diagrams and grinned. "This place has all the excitement of a library after hours."

Olivia sighed. "I don't know what's worse—the waiting or the actual dentist part."

Mia gestured to the corner where a sad-looking fake plant sat. "Hey, at least you've got that lovely plastic fern to look at."

The minutes dragged by, each one slower than the last. A soft classical tune played overhead, the kind of music that's supposed to relax you but only made Olivia more impatient.

Finally, after what felt like an eternity, the receptionist called her name. Olivia stood up dramatically, pretending she was about to enter a battle arena. "Wish me luck," she said, as if she were a gladiator heading into the lion's den.

Mia gave her a thumbs-up. "Don't let the drill defeat you!

18. As Riveting as Fishing Without Bait

Max and his dad sat by the lake, fishing poles in hand, staring at the still water. "You forgot the bait," Max said for the fourth time.

His dad sighed. "We'll just have to fish the old-fashioned way. With patience."

Max glanced at his dad, skeptical. "But how are the fish supposed to bite if there's no bait?"

"Maybe they'll admire the hook," his dad suggested with a grin.

The two of them sat in silence, their lines hanging limply in the water. "This is like playing basketball without a ball," Max muttered.

After an hour of absolutely nothing happening, Max laid down on the grass, staring up at the sky. "This has to be the most pointless activity ever. The fish are probably laughing at us."

His dad chuckled. “It’s not about catching fish. It’s about spending time together.”

Max frowned. “Well, I’d rather spend time actually fishing.”

19. As Intense as Sorting Pennies

Abby stared at the jar of pennies on the table, wondering how her life had come to this. “I’m about to sort pennies by year,” she said out loud, as if hearing it would make the task seem less ridiculous.

Her little brother, Liam, watched in disbelief. “Why?”

Abby shrugged. “Because... I need a hobby, I guess?”

For the next hour, she sifted through the jar, organizing the pennies into neat little piles, muttering the years under her breath like she was reciting an ancient spell. “1992... 1997... 2004...”

Liam, now thoroughly bored, asked, “Is this fun for you?”

Abby paused, staring at the tiny mountain of pennies she’d created. “It’s like... the slowest treasure hunt in history. Except instead of treasure, you find... more pennies.”

20. As Thrilling as Defrosting the Freezer

Jenny stared at her freezer, now filled with frost thick enough to build an igloo. "It’s time," she muttered, rolling up her sleeves.

Her roommate, Chloe, peeked around the corner. “You’re really going to defrost it? Good luck. We might need a flamethrower.”

Jenny grabbed a hairdryer and a plastic spatula. “No need. I’m going in.”

For the next hour, she blasted hot air at the ice, watching in painstakingly slow motion as it melted, drip by boring drip. Every few minutes, she’d chip away at the frost, feeling like an archaeologist digging for ancient treasures, only her treasure was frozen peas she'd forgotten about months ago.

Chloe sat on the couch, watching with a grin. "Riveting stuff."

Jenny shot her a look. "This is the most thrilling thing I've done all week. Can't you tell?"

After what felt like a lifetime, a giant chunk of ice finally fell with a dramatic *thud*. Jenny wiped her brow, exhausted but triumphant. "Victory!"

Chloe glanced at the still half-frozen freezer. "Yeah, you're halfway there.

21. As Edge-of-Your-Seat as Folding Laundry

Ben stared at the massive pile of laundry on his bed, as if it had grown larger since he last looked at it. "This is going to take forever," he groaned.

His girlfriend, Katie, leaned against the doorframe. "You act like you're climbing Everest. It's just clothes."

Ben held up a t-shirt, shaking his head. "No, this is an epic journey. One man versus a mountain of cotton and polyester."

Katie rolled her eyes. "You want help?"

"No, I have to face this challenge alone," Ben replied, dramatically folding the shirt as if it were a sacred ritual.

For the next half hour, Ben folded clothes at a snail's pace, occasionally pausing to critique his own folding technique. "I should've been a retail clerk. Look at these perfect lines!"

Katie chuckled. "You know what's funny? You're making it take longer."

Ben held up a pair of socks triumphantly. “True artistry can’t be rushed!”

22. As Wild as Untying a Knot in Your Shoelaces

Zoe stared at her tangled shoelaces like she was defusing a bomb. “How does this even happen?” she grumbled.

Her friend, Ava, watched with amusement. “You always do this. You’re like a walking knot machine.”

Zoe carefully tugged at one of the loops, but the knot only tightened. “This is harder than solving a Rubik’s cube,” she muttered.

“Need scissors?” Ava teased.

Zoe shook her head. “No way. This knot and I are in a battle of wills now.”

For the next ten minutes, Zoe twisted and pulled at the laces like she was performing some kind of shoe surgery. “I got this,” she kept saying, though her confidence was starting to waver.

Ava leaned in. “It’s like you’re negotiating with the laces.”

Zoe grinned. “They’ll crack eventually.”

Finally, after what felt like an eternity, the knot loosened, and Zoe pulled the laces free with a victorious cheer. “Ha! I win!”

Ava clapped sarcastically. “The real hero’s journey. You should write a memoir.”

23. As Enthralling as Watching a Fan Spin

Oliver lay on his bed, staring at the ceiling fan slowly rotating above him. “This is the most boring thing I’ve ever done,” he mumbled.

His sister, Lily, leaned in the doorway. “Why are you staring at the fan?”

Oliver shrugged. "I don't know. It's mesmerizing in a really boring way."

Lily crossed her arms. "You could, I don't know, do literally anything else?"

Oliver kept his eyes fixed on the fan. "But what if it does something cool? Like, what if it spins so fast it flies off the ceiling?"

Lily snorted. "Yeah, that's definitely going to happen."

For the next hour, Oliver stared at the fan, convinced that something exciting was *just* about to happen. But the fan kept spinning at its usual, predictable pace, never deviating, never wobbling.

Finally, Lily couldn't take it anymore. "I can't believe you're still watching that thing!"

Oliver sat up, stretching. "I'm training my patience."

Lily raised an eyebrow. "Or losing your mind."

24. As Dramatic as Waiting for a Website to Load on Dial-Up

Kyle sat in front of the computer, staring at the loading bar creeping across the screen. "This takes forever," he groaned.

His little brother, Liam, poked his head in the room. "Still loading?"

Kyle sighed. "It's been like five minutes. I could've built this website myself by now."

The whiny screech of the dial-up modem buzzed through the room as the page loaded one pixel at a time. "This is like watching a turtle swim through molasses," Kyle muttered.

Liam snickered. "What's the rush?"

Kyle shook his head. "I'm trying to download a picture for my report, but at this rate, I'll be retired before it finishes."

Finally, after an eternity, the page loaded in its grainy glory. Kyle clapped sarcastically. "Woo! I can finally see a low-res picture of a dinosaur!"

Liam grinned. "Good luck getting the next page to load."

25. As Heart-Pounding as Reorganizing the Junk Drawer

Rachel opened the junk drawer in the kitchen and sighed at the chaos inside. Pens, rubber bands, batteries, and takeout menus were jumbled together in a mess that defied logic. "How did it get this bad?"

Her friend Mia, sitting at the counter, laughed. "It's like the Bermuda Triangle in there. Stuff goes in but never comes out."

Rachel pulled out a random tangle of wires. "I don't even know what half of this is. I swear this wire came with a VCR we haven't had in years."

For the next hour, she sorted through the drawer, carefully dividing everything into categories that would probably only last a week before it all ended up jumbled again. "This is like sorting puzzle pieces where none of them fit," she muttered.

Mia watched in mock horror. "Careful. If you remove the wrong thing, the whole drawer might collapse."

Rachel finally managed to wrangle the drawer into some semblance of order, wiping her hands like she'd just completed a major home renovation. "Done!"

Mia peered inside. "Give it a week. The junk will rise again."

26. As Captivating as Watching Paint Dry

Sophia and her dad stood in front of the freshly painted wall, staring at it like it was a piece of modern art. "Now we just wait for it to dry," her dad said, as if this was the most exciting event on the planet.

Sophia folded her arms. "This is the most boring thing I've ever done."

Her dad shrugged. "Patience is a virtue."

Sophia rolled her eyes. "You say that because you're not the one staring at the wall."

For the next half-hour, they both sat there, watching as the paint slowly, agonizingly dried. Every once in a while, Sophia would ask, "Is it dry yet?" only to be met with a slow shake of the head.

Finally, after what felt like an eternity, the paint dried. Sophia sighed in relief. "Finally!"

Her dad grinned. "See? Patience pays off."

Sophia stared at him, deadpan. "Next time, I'm using a blow dryer."

27. As Gripping as Standing in Line at the DMV

Greg stared at the long line snaking through the DMV like it was a never-ending rollercoaster of misery. "This is going to take years," he muttered.

His friend Jake, standing next to him, smirked. "Oh come on, man, this is where all the excitement happens. You never know when they'll call your number! It's like bingo, but with more paperwork."

Greg sighed and glanced at the ticket in his hand: Number 103. The sign above the counter blinked: 45. "They're not even halfway."

For the next hour, they stood in line, the dull hum of conversations and shuffling feet creating a background soundtrack of bureaucratic boredom. Occasionally, someone would sigh dramatically or groan when their number wasn't called.

Jake leaned in and whispered, "You think they do this on purpose? Like, they make us suffer so the experience of getting your license renewed feels like an achievement?"

Greg chuckled. "I feel like I should get a trophy for surviving this."

Finally, after what felt like a lifetime, the sign blinked: 103. Greg jumped up like he'd just won the lottery. "That's me!"

Jake clapped. "You did it, man. I'm so proud."

28. As Exciting as Waiting for Bread to Toast

Mia stood in front of the toaster, staring at the two slices of bread slowly transforming into toast. "This is taking forever," she groaned.

Her brother, Luke, sat at the table, grinning. "You know, watching toast toast is a real art form. You've got to appreciate the subtle changes, the slow browning..."

Mia rolled her eyes. "You're ridiculous. I just want breakfast."

For the next few minutes, she continued to stare at the toaster, convinced that her impatient gaze would somehow speed up the process. But the toaster remained defiant, toasting at its usual, unhurried pace.

Luke leaned in. "Maybe if you chant, 'Toast, toast, toast,' it'll go faster."

Mia shot him a look. "That's not how science works."

Finally, with a dramatic *pop*, the toaster released her golden-brown bread. Mia grabbed the toast triumphantly. "Finally! Victory is mine."

Luke clapped slowly. "You've conquered the toaster. I'm in awe."

29. As Electrifying as Waiting for a Kettle to Boil

Jess stared at the kettle, willing it to boil faster. "Come on, come on..."

Her roommate, Alex, wandered into the kitchen and raised an eyebrow. "Why are you just standing there?"

Jess sighed dramatically. "I'm waiting for the kettle to boil. It's like the slowest thing on Earth."

Alex laughed. "You know what they say, 'A watched pot never boils.'"

Jess shot him a look. "That's not helpful."

For the next several minutes, Jess kept staring at the kettle like it was a ticking time bomb. Every tiny hiss or bubble made her jump, thinking it was finally ready, but the water remained stubbornly lukewarm.

Alex leaned against the counter, amused. "You could, I don't know, do something else while you wait?"

Jess shook her head. "No. I've committed to this."

Finally, the kettle started to whistle, and Jess let out a triumphant cheer. "Yes! Boiling water!"

Alex clapped sarcastically. "A monumental achievement in human history."

30. As Engaging as Sorting a Box of Mixed-Up Puzzle Pieces

Charlotte stared at the box of puzzle pieces dumped onto the table, each piece jumbled together in a chaotic mess. "This is going to take hours," she groaned.

Her friend, Maya, grabbed a piece and examined it. "Why did you buy a 5,000-piece puzzle? Are you a masochist?"

Charlotte shrugged. "I thought it'd be fun. But now it's like I'm trying to solve a mystery where none of the clues make sense."

For the next hour, they sorted through the pieces, occasionally finding one that looked like it *might* belong somewhere, only to be foiled by its lack of fit. "It's like trying to put together a Rubik's cube in the dark," Maya muttered.

Charlotte nodded. "This puzzle is mocking us."

Finally, after what felt like an eternity, they managed to sort the pieces into rough categories. Charlotte leaned back in her chair. "Well, that only took forever."

Maya laughed. "Next time, we're doing a puzzle with, like, 20 pieces. Tops."

31. As Riveting as Watching Water Freeze

Tim filled the ice cube tray, carefully sliding it into the freezer. "And now we wait," he said, staring into the frosty abyss.

His sister, Claire, walked by and raised an eyebrow. "You're watching ice freeze? Is this what your life has come to?"

Tim shrugged. "It's a science experiment. I want to see how long it takes."

Claire rolled her eyes. "You're going to be standing there for a while."

For the next hour, Tim checked the freezer every ten minutes, convinced that he could speed up the freezing process with sheer willpower. "It's getting colder," he announced proudly, though the tray still sloshed with liquid water.

Claire laughed. "You're like one of those people who watches a pot of water and wonders why it doesn't boil."

Tim waved her off. "This is different. This is *ice*."

Finally, after what felt like an eternity, the water began to freeze. Tim grinned triumphantly. “See? Science!”

Claire clapped slowly. “You should get a Nobel Prize for this.”

32. As Intense as Changing the Batteries in the TV Remote

Sam pressed the power button on the TV remote, but nothing happened. He tried again, and again. “Great. The batteries are dead,” he grumbled.

His roommate, Dave, looked over. “Guess you’ll have to get up and change them.”

Sam sighed dramatically. “I was not prepared for this level of physical exertion today.”

Dave chuckled. “It’s literally the easiest thing you’ll do all week.”

Sam trudged over to the junk drawer, where a chaotic mess of batteries awaited him. After sorting through a pile of mismatched sizes, he finally found two AA batteries. “Success!”

For the next few minutes, Sam struggled to open the back of the remote, as if it were a puzzle designed by an evil genius. “Why do they make these things so hard to open?”

Dave smirked. “Maybe they’re trying to make sure only the worthy can wield the power of television.”

Finally, after what felt like an epic battle, Sam swapped out the batteries and pressed the power button. The TV blinked to life. “Victory!” he shouted.

Dave clapped. “You truly are a hero.”

33. As Fascinating as Organizing the Spice Rack

Lila stared at the chaotic mess of spice jars in her kitchen cupboard. “Why do I have three bottles of cumin?” she muttered.

Her roommate, Jess, walked by and glanced at the mess. “I think your spice rack has become self-aware.”

Lila sighed. “It’s time. I’m going to organize this thing once and for all.”

For the next hour, she pulled out every single jar, lining them up on the counter in some sort of vague order. “Why do I have so much cinnamon? I don’t even like cinnamon.”

Jess leaned against the counter, watching in amusement. “This is your Everest. You’ll never conquer it.”

Lila shot her a look. “I will conquer this spice rack, and it will bow before me.”

After what felt like an eternity of sorting, labeling, and reorganizing, the spice rack finally looked like it belonged in a professional kitchen. Lila wiped her hands dramatically. “Done.”

Jess peered at the neat rows of spices. “You know, in a week, it’ll all be a mess again.”

Lila sighed. “Yeah, probably.”

34. As Thrilling as Waiting for a Slow Printer

Emma hit "print" and waited. And waited. The printer made a low hum, its gears slowly grinding to life like a sloth waking up from a nap. “This is going to take forever,” she muttered.

Her brother Jack poked his head in the door. “What are you printing? A novel?”

Emma sighed. “Just one page, but at this rate, I might as well be printing the entire Encyclopedia Britannica.”

For the next several minutes, the printer spat out the page one agonizing line at a time, as if it were teasing her with its slowness. Emma leaned against the desk, staring at it like she could will it to go faster.

Jack laughed. "You look like you're waiting for a miracle."

Emma grinned sarcastically. "This is the most exciting thing I've done all day."

Finally, with a triumphant beep, the printer finished. Emma held up the page dramatically. "Victory!"

Jack clapped slowly. "What a journey."

35. As Adventurous as Trying to Find the End of the Tape

Liam sat at his desk, glaring at the roll of clear tape in front of him. "Where is it?" he muttered, running his fingers around the edge.

His friend Noah walked by, chuckling. "Still trying to find the end of the tape? That's a classic struggle."

Liam grumbled. "It's like trying to find buried treasure, but the treasure doesn't want to be found."

For the next several minutes, Liam scratched and tugged at the tape, getting more frustrated with every pass. "This is like trying to solve a mystery where the culprit is invisible."

Noah sat down next to him, amused. "Need a magnifying glass?"

Finally, after what felt like an eternity, Liam found the tiny, elusive edge and pulled it free with a shout of triumph. "I did it!"

Noah clapped. "You've conquered the world's greatest foe: clear tape."

36. As Exhilarating as Untangling Christmas Lights

Rachel opened the box of Christmas lights, only to find a tangled mess that looked more like a pile of spaghetti than holiday decor. "Why does this happen every year?" she sighed.

Her roommate, Sarah, peered over her shoulder. "Because you put them away like a maniac last year."

Rachel groaned. "This is like trying to untangle a ball of yarn that a cat's been playing with for hours."

For the next hour, she slowly worked through the knots, tugging and twisting the lights in every direction. Occasionally, she'd make progress, only to have a new knot appear, mocking her efforts.

Sarah grabbed a strand and started to help. "It's like a puzzle, but there's no picture on the box."

Finally, after what felt like an epic battle, they managed to free the last strand. Rachel held it up like a trophy. "We did it! Christmas is saved!"

Sarah clapped. "Only took you an hour."

37. As Gripping as Waiting for Software to Install

Jason clicked "Install" and leaned back in his chair, watching as the progress bar slowly inched forward. "This is going to take forever," he muttered.

His roommate, Mark, wandered into the room. "You waiting for your software to install? That's always a thrill."

Jason sighed. "It's like watching a snail run a marathon."

For the next several minutes, Jason sat there, watching the percentage tick up by fractions. Every time it seemed to speed up, it would suddenly stall at a random number like 73%. "Come on..." he groaned.

Mark laughed. "You know, you could do something else while you wait."

Jason shook his head. "No. I need to be here. I need to see this through."

Finally, after what felt like an eternity, the installation finished, and Jason threw his arms in the air. "Yes! It's done!"

Mark clapped sarcastically. "You survived the ordeal. I'm impressed."

38. As Action-Packed as Peeling a Sticker Off a New Item

Megan stared at the stubborn sticker on her new mug. "Why do they use superglue for these things?" she muttered, scratching at the edge.

Her friend Emily sat nearby, laughing. "You're battling the ultimate enemy: stubborn stickers."

Megan groaned. "It's like they don't want you to ever use the product. I'm going to spend more time peeling this off than I'll ever spend drinking coffee from it."

For the next few minutes, Megan scratched and tugged at the sticker, which seemed determined to stay stuck forever. "This is like trying to peel off a band-aid without any of the satisfaction."

Finally, after what felt like ages, she managed to peel off the last bit, though it left behind a sticky residue. Megan held up the mug triumphantly. "Victory!"

Emily clapped. "You've overcome the impossible."

39. As Enthralling as Watching Your Phone Update

Katie clicked "Update Now" on her phone and set it down on the table. "Well, there goes my next half hour," she muttered.

Her brother, Mike, laughed. "Ah, the old 'watch your phone update' game. Always a good time."

Katie groaned. "Why does it take so long? It's like my phone is downloading the entire internet."

For the next several minutes, she stared at the progress bar, which seemed to be moving slower than molasses. Every time it hit a new milestone, she'd get a small spark of hope, only for it to stall again.

Mike leaned in. "You know, you could just leave it and do something else."

Katie shook her head. "No, I have to make sure it doesn't die in the middle of the update."

Finally, after what felt like an eternity, the update finished, and her phone rebooted. Katie grinned. "It's alive!"

Mike clapped. "What a rollercoaster of emotions."

40. As Edge-of-Your-Seat as Filling Out a Tax Form

Josh sat at his desk, staring at the tax form in front of him. "Why is this so complicated?" he groaned.

His girlfriend, Ella, looked over his shoulder. "Because taxes are designed to be as confusing as possible. It's like a riddle wrapped in an enigma, buried under a mountain of paperwork."

Josh sighed. "This is like solving a puzzle where all the pieces are the same shape and color."

For the next hour, he slowly filled out the form, double-checking every line and number as if he were defusing a bomb. "One wrong move and I'll owe the government my soul," he muttered.

Ella laughed. "You're being dramatic."

Finally, after what felt like an eternity, Josh filled in the last blank and set the form down with a dramatic flourish. "Done! I survived tax season!"

Ella clapped slowly. "You're a true hero."

41. As Captivating as Ironing a Shirt

Samantha stared at the wrinkled shirt on the ironing board. “Why do I hate ironing so much?” she muttered, grabbing the iron.

Her friend, Leah, sat on the couch, laughing. “Because it’s literally the most boring thing in the world.”

Samantha groaned. “It’s like painting a fence, but instead of creating something, you’re just erasing wrinkles.”

For the next several minutes, she ironed the shirt, carefully smoothing out each crease with all the enthusiasm of someone watching paint dry. “This is the pinnacle of excitement,” she muttered sarcastically.

Leah grinned. “You should enter an ironing competition. I bet you’d win.”

Finally, after what felt like an eternity, the shirt was wrinkle-free. Samantha held it up triumphantly. “Done!”

Leah clapped slowly. “You’ve achieved greatness.”

42. As Stimulating as Folding Laundry

Lily sat on her bed, surrounded by a mountain of clean laundry. “Why does it feel like I’ve been folding clothes for years?” she grumbled.

Her roommate, Zoe, walked by and smirked. “Because folding laundry is like trying to empty an ocean with a spoon. It’s never-ending.”

Lily sighed. “This is the least rewarding chore ever. I fold it, put it away, and tomorrow it’s right back where it started.”

For the next several minutes, she methodically folded t-shirts, socks, and towels, each one feeling like a small piece of her soul was being packed away. “I think this laundry pile is multiplying,” she muttered.

Zoe leaned against the doorframe. “You know, you could just live out of the laundry basket. That’s what I do.”

Lily chuckled. “Tempting, but then I’d never find matching socks.”

Finally, after what felt like an eternity, she folded the last item and collapsed onto the bed. “Done. I’ve conquered the laundry monster.”

Zoe clapped. “You’re a true laundry warrior.”

44. As Engaging as Watching a Website Load on Dial-Up

Mark clicked on a link and waited as the familiar sound of the dial-up modem screeched from his computer. “This is going to take forever,” he groaned.

His sister, Amy, laughed. “Dial-up internet is like watching paint dry, but with more frustration.”

Mark sighed. “It’s like the internet is traveling by horse and buggy.”

For the next several minutes, the page loaded pixel by pixel, each new section appearing with excruciating slowness. Every time it seemed like it was almost done, it would freeze again, leaving Mark staring at the spinning loading icon.

Amy leaned over his shoulder. “Remember when we thought this was fast?”

Mark rolled his eyes. “Yeah, it was a simpler time.”

Finally, after what felt like an eternity, the webpage fully loaded. Mark threw his hands in the air. “We made it!”

Amy clapped. “What a thrilling journey.

45. As Heart-Pounding as Refilling the Soap Dispenser

Kara stared at the empty soap dispenser on the bathroom counter. “How does this always run out when I’m in a hurry?” she muttered.

Her brother, Luke, walked by and raised an eyebrow. “Because the soap dispenser is an agent of chaos, bent on ruining your day.”

Kara groaned. "It's like a never-ending battle between me and household chores."

For the next several minutes, she carefully refilled the dispenser, trying not to spill soap everywhere. "Why is this so stressful?" she muttered.

Luke laughed. "Because you know if you overfill it, it's going to spill and be a sticky mess."

Finally, after what felt like an eternity, Kara screwed the cap back on and wiped the counter clean. "Done. The soap has been tamed."

Luke clapped. "You've conquered the sudsy beast."

46. As Exciting as Putting New Batteries in the Smoke Detector

Jane stood on a chair, staring up at the smoke detector with its annoying, intermittent beeps. "Why do these things only start beeping in the middle of the night?" she grumbled.

Her husband, Dan, handed her the batteries. "Because they like to remind you they exist at the worst possible moments."

Jane sighed. "It's like a little electronic reminder that chaos lurks around every corner."

For the next few minutes, she fumbled with the cover, trying to pry it open without breaking it. "Why are these things so hard to open? They're like little Fort Knoxes."

Dan chuckled. "Probably to make sure only the truly determined can change the batteries."

Finally, after what felt like an eternity, Jane managed to change the batteries and reassemble the smoke detector. She hopped off the chair with a grin. "No more beeping!"

Dan clapped. "You've silenced the enemy. Well done."

47. As Suspenseful as Watching a YouTube Ad You Can't Skip

Charlie clicked on a YouTube video, only to be met with the dreaded words: "Your video will play after this ad."

He groaned. "Why is it always the longest ads that you can't skip?"

His sister, Emma, sat beside him, laughing. "Because they know you have no choice. It's like they're holding your video hostage."

Charlie sighed. "It's like being stuck in a never-ending infomercial."

For the next thirty seconds, they endured a painfully dull ad for a product neither of them cared about. "I think I've aged ten years waiting for this to end," Charlie muttered.

Emma chuckled. "This is the true test of patience."

Finally, the ad ended, and the video began to play. Charlie grinned. "Freedom!"

Emma clapped. "You survived the ultimate YouTube challenge."

48. As Tense as Waiting for a Traffic Light to Change

Ben sat in his car, staring at the red light in front of him. "Why does this light take forever to change?" he muttered.

His friend, Max, sat in the passenger seat, smirking. "Because traffic lights are designed to make you question your life choices."

Ben sighed. "It's like they're purposely mocking me."

For the next few minutes, they sat in silence as the light remained stubbornly red. Every time Ben thought it might change, it stayed the same, leaving him stuck in place.

Max chuckled. "You could probably write a novel while we wait for this light."

Finally, after what felt like an eternity, the light turned green, and Ben hit the gas. "Victory!"

Max clapped. "You've conquered the world's slowest traffic light."

49. As Captivating as Deleting Spam Emails

Ella sat at her computer, scrolling through a mountain of unread emails. "Why do I get so much spam?" she muttered.

Her coworker, Sam, leaned over her shoulder. "Because the internet loves to fill your inbox with things you'll never read."

Ella sighed. "It's like a never-ending battle between me and the delete button."

For the next several minutes, she methodically deleted email after email, her finger hovering over the mouse like a seasoned warrior in the heat of battle.

Sam chuckled. "You're like the Terminator, but for spam."

Finally, after what felt like an eternity, Ella cleared her inbox and leaned back in her chair. "Done."

Sam clapped. "You've defeated the spam overlords. Well done."

50. As Thrilling as Watching Paint Dry

Steve dipped his brush into the paint can and slowly applied the first coat to the wall. "This is going to be a long day," he muttered.

His wife, Lisa, stood nearby, grinning. "Watching paint dry is one of life's great pleasures."

Steve sighed. "It's like the ultimate test of patience. You work so hard to put it on, and then you just... wait."

For the next several minutes, Steve watched the paint slowly dry, the wet sheen fading as the color deepened. Occasionally, he'd poke the wall with his finger, only to find it still sticky.

Lisa laughed. "You look like you're watching grass grow."

Steve smirked. "At least grass grows on its own. This requires supervision."

Finally, after what felt like an eternity, the paint dried, and Steve stood back to admire his work. "Done. It's dry."

Lisa clapped. "What an exhilarating journey.

51. As Riveting as Waiting for Toast to Pop

Tom placed two slices of bread in the toaster and stared at it as if willing it to speed up. "Why does toast always take forever when you're starving?" he groaned.

His roommate, Jake, wandered into the kitchen. "Because toast is nature's way of teaching us patience. It's like waiting for a miracle."

Tom sighed. "It's like the bread's on a mini-vacation in there, just chilling while I'm about to die of hunger."

For the next several minutes, Tom hovered near the toaster, waiting for that magical 'pop' sound. Every few seconds, he'd peek in, only to find the bread slowly browning.

Jake smirked. "If you watch it too hard, it'll never pop."

Finally, with a loud 'pop,' the toast launched itself from the toaster. Tom grabbed it triumphantly. "Success! Breakfast is served."

Jake clapped. "You've conquered the toasting gods."

52. As Electrifying as Untangling Headphone Wires

Jess stared at the tangled mess of headphone wires in her hand. "Why do they always end up like this?" she muttered.

Her friend, Molly, chuckled. "Because headphone wires have a mind of their own. They're like little knots of chaos."

Jess sighed. "It's like they tangle themselves just for fun. I didn't even move them!"

For the next several minutes, Jess painstakingly worked to untangle the knots, her fingers twisting and turning like a master puzzle solver. Each knot seemed more complicated than the last, as if the wires were actively resisting her efforts.

Molly smirked. "I think those things have more knots than a sailor's rope."

Finally, after what felt like an eternity, Jess untangled the last knot and let out a triumphant yell. "Victory!"

Molly clapped. "You've defeated the headphone beast."

53. As Engaging as Waiting for a Software Update

Brian clicked "Install" and immediately regretted it. "Why do updates take so long?" he groaned, staring at the progress bar that moved at a glacial pace.

His sister, Claire, leaned over. "Because updates are the computer's way of reminding you that it's in control."

Brian sighed. "It's like the computer's telling me, 'You thought you were going to use me today? Ha!'"

For the next several minutes, Brian sat there, watching the progress bar inch forward. Every time it seemed like it was close to finishing, it'd stall again, stuck at 99%.

Claire smirked. "It's teasing you. It knows you're waiting."

Finally, after what felt like an eternity, the update finished, and the computer restarted. Brian threw his hands up. "At last! Freedom!"

Claire clapped. "You've survived the ultimate tech challenge."

54. As Tense as Waiting for Water to Boil

Samantha stood by the stove, watching the pot of water. "Why does water take forever to boil when you're in a hurry?" she grumbled.

Her partner, Alex, walked by and smiled. "Because water likes to mess with you. It knows you're waiting."

Samantha sighed. "It's like the bubbles are staging a rebellion."

For the next several minutes, she stared at the pot, waiting for the first signs of boiling. Every now and then, a tiny bubble would rise to the surface, taunting her. "Come on! Just boil already!" she muttered.

Alex leaned against the counter. "You know the saying: A watched pot never boils."

Finally, after what felt like an eternity, the water began to bubble furiously. Samantha let out a cheer. "We have lift-off!"

Alex clapped. "You've defeated the water's passive-aggressive behavior."

55. As Thrilling as Watching a Clock Tick

Lena sat in the classroom, staring at the clock on the wall. "Why does time slow down during the last five minutes of class?" she whispered to her friend, Jamie.

Jamie shrugged. "Because clocks are evil. They know you're waiting for freedom."

Lena sighed. "It's like the second hand is stuck in molasses."

For the next several minutes, they watched the clock as it slowly, painfully, ticked from one second to the next. Every tick felt like an eternity, as if time itself had decided to rebel against them.

Jamie smirked. “This is the slowest countdown to freedom I’ve ever seen.”

Finally, after what felt like an eternity, the bell rang. Lena jumped out of her seat. “We made it!”

Jamie clapped. “We survived the longest five minutes of our lives.

56. As Exciting as Watching Grass Grow

Max flopped onto the lawn chair, staring at the patch of grass in his backyard. “You know, this is as exciting as watching grass grow,” he said, feigning a dramatic sigh. His best friend, Jake, was sprawled next to him, squinting at the sun. “You mean it’s exhilarating?” Jake shot back, rolling his eyes. “My heart can barely take it!”

Determined to make this a riveting event, Max leaped up. “Let’s document this epic moment in history!” He grabbed his phone and began narrating like a nature documentary host. “And here we have the majestic grass, known scientifically as *Grasstasticus boringus*,” he announced, pointing dramatically at the green blades swaying in the breeze. “Look how it stands tall and proud, just waiting for... something...anything!”

Jake couldn’t contain his laughter. “You know, I think I just felt a blade grow! Quick, get the camera!”

“Wait! I need to adjust my angle for the perfect shot!” Max replied, crouching low. “And look at this one! This is *Grassicus Supremus*! Truly, the king of all grasses!”

As they continued their absurd commentary, they imagined the grass’s daily life. “Every morning, it wakes up to the sound of the birds, pondering the meaning of life,” Max said, putting his hand on his chin in deep thought. “It probably asks itself, ‘Why was I chosen to be so green and luscious?’”

Suddenly, Jake pointed. “Wait! Is that a bug? A grasshopper, perhaps?”

Max whipped out his phone. “Breaking news: a grasshopper has entered the field!” He zoomed in dramatically. “This is the moment we’ve all been waiting for! Will it eat the grass? Will it befriend it? The tension is palpable!”

They cracked up at their own silliness, creating wild scenarios where the grass and grasshopper entered a life-or-death negotiation. “What if the grasshopper wants to claim the grass for its own? A turf war!”

As the sun began to set, casting a golden glow over their yard, Jake turned to Max. “I’ve gotta admit, this was pretty thrilling. Who knew grass could be so riveting?”

Max grinned. “Next time, let’s schedule a grass-growing watch party! We can invite everyone!”

“Bring the popcorn!” Jake replied, laughing. “I want to see if we can get a blade to break the speed record!”

57. As Boring as Filling Out Forms

Derek slumped at his desk, staring blankly at a stack of forms that seemed to multiply like rabbits. “This is as exciting as watching paint dry…in slow motion!” he muttered. His coworker Lisa peeked over her cubicle, smirking. “Oh, come on! It’s not that bad. You’re on the thrill ride of administrative tasks!”

Derek raised an eyebrow. “Yeah, if your idea of a thrill ride is filling out the ‘employee satisfaction survey’ for the fourth time this year. I feel like I’m in a groundhog day nightmare!”

Lisa chuckled and pulled up a chair. “Let’s spice things up! How about we create the ultimate game out of this?”

“Game? How?” Derek asked, intrigued despite himself.

“Every time you fill out a field correctly, you get a point! But if you make a mistake... penalties!” she said with a wicked grin.

“Penalties? Like what? A surprise dance party in the break room?” Derek joked, waving a hand dramatically.

“No, even worse! You have to repeat the phrase ‘I love filling out forms’ five times in a row at the top of your lungs!”

Derek pretended to shudder. “The horror! You’re a true villain!”

With that, he picked up his pen and began filling out the first form. “Here we go! ‘Name: Derek Smith.’ Point for me! Now, ‘Address...’”

As he filled in each line, they began to exaggerate every word. “Address! Point! Phone number! Point! At this rate, I’ll have enough points to win a trip to Hawaii!”

“Or maybe just a complimentary pen,” Lisa retorted, giggling.

Every time Derek made a mistake, they burst into laughter. “Oh no! You miswrote your phone number! Five times!” Lisa teased, trying to catch her breath as Derek dramatically threw his head back in defeat.

Finally, after what felt like an eternity, he completed the last form. “I’m free!” he shouted, dramatically tossing his pen into the air. “Let the confetti rain down!”

Lisa laughed. “Congratulations! You’ve survived the boredom of paperwork! What’s next? A wild expedition to the break room for coffee?”

“Only if it’s an adventure worth documenting!” Derek replied with a wink.

If you like these styles, I can create more! Just let me know

58. As Gripping as Watching a Snail Race

Samantha stood at the edge of her backyard, peering down at the two snails on the patio. "This is as gripping as watching a snail race," she declared dramatically. Her friend Ben, lying on the grass, raised an eyebrow. "You mean you're not thrilled? This is high-stakes entertainment!"

Samantha squatted down, eyes wide. "Do you feel the tension? This is where champions are made!" She pointed at the snails. "On the left, we have Turbo Tim, known for his legendary speed. On the right, we have Slowpoke Sally, the underdog everyone doubts!"

"Will Turbo Tim finally outrun Slowpoke Sally?" Ben asked, stifling laughter. "Or will she pull off the ultimate upset?"

Samantha clapped her hands. "Ready...set...go!"

The snails barely moved. In fact, they looked more like they were contemplating their life choices. "Look at them go! What a fierce competition!" Samantha exclaimed, leaning closer as if she were watching the Olympics.

After what felt like an eternity, Turbo Tim inched forward, while Slowpoke Sally remained still. "What's this? An unexpected strategy from Slowpoke Sally? Could she be playing possum?"

Ben cracked up. "I didn't know snails could employ psychological tactics!"

As the snails continued their slow-motion standoff, Samantha narrated their inner thoughts. "Turbo Tim is thinking, 'I can't lose! The world is watching!' Meanwhile, Slowpoke Sally is pondering the meaning of life, wondering if it's really worth racing at all."

"Maybe she just wants to stop and smell the roses," Ben suggested, gesturing to the flowers nearby.

"Exactly! Life's not all about winning!" Samantha proclaimed, raising her hands dramatically. "It's about enjoying the little things!"

Just then, a leaf fluttered down and landed on Slowpoke Sally. "Oh no! An unexpected obstacle!" Samantha shouted, feigning shock. "Can she overcome it? Will she be able to dodge the leafy menace?"

In a surprising twist, both snails suddenly perked up and began to move—well, more like a slight shift. "It's a miracle! They're both racing!" Ben cheered, unable to hold back his laughter.

Finally, after a slow crawl that felt like watching molasses drip, Turbo Tim crossed an imaginary finish line. "Victory! Turbo Tim takes the crown!" Samantha shouted. "But truly, they are both winners in our hearts!"

"Next time, let's do this with actual racing snails," Ben suggested, still giggling.

59. As Captivating as Sorting Your Socks

Lila sat on her bedroom floor, surrounded by a mountain of mismatched socks. "This is as captivating as sorting your socks," she sighed, holding up a bright pink sock with a unicorn on it. Her friend Zoe burst into laughter. "Oh come on! The sock sorting championship has officially begun!"

"Right? The stakes couldn't be higher!" Lila replied, pretending to be a sports commentator. "We have Team Rainbow Unicorns going up against Team Boring Black!"

Zoe grabbed a polka-dotted sock. "And here we have a rogue polka-dot, not affiliated with any team! The scandal!"

"An interloper!" Lila gasped, clutching her heart. "How could this happen? The sock community is in turmoil!"

As they dove into the sock chaos, they made up elaborate backstories for each sock. "This one here," Lila said, holding up a striped sock, "was a brave adventurer, traveling far and wide. But alas, it lost its partner in the sock wilderness!"

Zoe pointed to a pair of fuzzy socks. "These two are conjoined twins! They stick together no matter what, always facing the world in cozy solidarity!"

Lila threw her head back, laughing. "And this one! A lone warrior who fought valiantly in the washing machine battles, emerging victorious, yet forever changed!"

With each sock, their storytelling escalated to absurd levels. "And here's a sock that went on a journey to the dryer, only to return with a newfound sense of purpose!"

Finally, after what felt like an epic saga, they sorted the socks into neat piles. "We've done it! The great sock sorting is complete!" Lila declared, arms raised in triumph.

"Now what do we do with our newfound power?" Zoe asked, grinning.

"Throw a sock party, of course! Everyone's invited!" Lila responded, laughing. "But they have to wear mismatched socks to get in!"

60. As Exciting as Watching Your Phone Load a Video

Jamie sat on the couch, staring intently at her phone. "This is as exciting as watching your phone load a video," she said, her eyes glued to the loading bar. "I feel like I'm in a suspense thriller!"

Her friend Tim plopped down beside her, chuckling. "I bet this is where they reveal the shocking twist!"

Jamie leaned closer. "Will it load? Or will it forever be stuck in loading limbo?" The loading bar crawled across the screen like a snail on a leisurely stroll.

"I can't take this! It's like a cliffhanger that lasts forever!" Tim exclaimed dramatically, throwing his hands up. "What if the video is a cat failing at jumping? We may never know!"

As the seconds ticked by, Jamie pretended to narrate the scene. "And here we have the loading bar, moving at an astonishing pace of...a millimeter every minute! The tension is palpable!"

"Will it make it to the finish line? The world is watching!" Tim added, leaning closer.

Finally, the bar inched closer to the end. "It's coming! Can you feel the excitement?" Jamie shouted, her voice rising. "What will we discover on the other side?"

With a dramatic flourish, the video finally loaded. "It's alive!" Jamie cheered, pumping her fist in the air. "We made it! The video is here!"

Tim laughed, shaking his head. "All that suspense for...a cat falling off a couch! The real twist was the loading time!"

"Honestly, I think the loading was more exciting than the video," Jamie admitted, still grinning. "We should charge admission for that rollercoaster ride!"

"I'd pay double for that thrill," Tim replied, wiping away tears of laughter. "Now, what's next? Watching the credits roll?"

61. As Exciting as Watching Your Hair Dry

Jessica stood in front of the bathroom mirror, her hair dripping wet. "This is as exciting as watching your hair dry," she declared, pouting. Her friend Mia burst into laughter. "Oh, come on! You're living on the edge!"

Jessica rolled her eyes. "Living on the edge of boredom, maybe!" She picked up her blow dryer. "What if we turn this into an epic adventure?"

Mia raised an eyebrow. "How? By creating a dramatic story around the drying process?"

"Exactly!" Jessica said, flipping her hair dramatically. "Behold, the tale of Hairius Maximus, hero of the bathroom kingdom!"

As she began blow-drying, she narrated. "With each blast of hot air, Hairius fights against the evil Dampness, determined to save the day!" She pointed the dryer like a sword, making heroic sound effects.

Mia joined in. "But wait! The evil Dampness fights back, swirling around Hairius with all its might!"

"Dampness can't win!" Jessica shouted, pointing the dryer more forcefully. "With every gust, Hairius grows stronger! Look at that volume!"

"Unbelievable! Will he conquer the waves?" Mia asked, pretending to lean forward in suspense.

Finally, Jessica set down the dryer and flipped her hair again, now mostly dry. "The battle is won! Hairius Maximus stands victorious!"

Mia clapped. "Bravo! You're a true warrior of the bathroom!"

Jessica grinned. "And look at my shiny locks! I'm ready for the grand ball!" She struck a pose. "All hail the queen of dry hair!"

"Next time, let's add a theme song!" Mia suggested, laughing.

"I'm thinking epic orchestra," Jessica said. "With dramatic violin solos as the climax!"

As they both cackled, Jessica picked up her hairbrush. "But first, we must untangle the evil knots! This could take a while!"

Mia pretended to gasp. "Not the knots! They're the ultimate foe!"

"I know!" Jessica said, her eyes wide. "But Hairius Maximus will prevail! Onward, to the styling victory!"

62. As Boring as Watching Your Bread Toast

Ethan stared at the toaster, watching a slice of bread slowly turn brown. "This is as boring as watching your bread toast," he sighed. His friend Zoe snorted, trying not to laugh. “What a thrill! The bread Olympics have begun!”

Ethan leaned closer, eyes wide with mock seriousness. “What if this is the moment we’ve all been waiting for? The toast of the century!”

Zoe chuckled, “Will it be perfectly golden? Or will it suffer the fate of burnt toast?”

“The stakes couldn’t be higher!” Ethan replied dramatically. “The toast has dreams, hopes, and aspirations!”

As they waited, Ethan pretended to be a sports commentator. “And here we have a stunning contender! Look at that browning action! Can you feel the intensity?”

Zoe bit her lip to hold back laughter. “I feel it! The tension is palpable! The audience is on the edge of their seats!”

“Just look at that crust! Will it be crispy enough to satisfy the crowd?” Ethan exclaimed, his eyes glued to the toaster.

Finally, the toaster popped, and Ethan leaped back. “It’s alive! We have toast!”

Zoe burst into laughter. “Oh my gosh! It’s a miracle! What a dramatic performance!”

Ethan dramatically lifted the toast like a trophy. “This is it! The culmination of our breakfast dreams!”

Zoe rolled her eyes, still giggling. “You realize we’re cheering for bread, right?”

“Not just any bread!” Ethan said, taking a triumphant bite. “This is toasted perfection! A work of art!”

“Next time, let’s have an award ceremony!” Zoe suggested. “Best supporting role goes to...the butter!”

Ethan laughed, shaking his head. "And best drama goes to...my patience!"

63. As Thrilling as Watching Water Boil

Liam stood in the kitchen, staring at a pot of water on the stove. "This is as thrilling as watching water boil," he announced dramatically. His sister Emma peeked over, smirking. "Oh, the excitement! What an adventure!"

Liam picked up a wooden spoon, raising it like a microphone. "Ladies and gentlemen, welcome to the epic showdown of the ages: The Boil-Off!"

Emma giggled. "Will it be a slow, painful demise, or a triumphant bubbling victory?"

"Only time will tell!" Liam replied, glancing at the pot. "Look at that water! So calm and collected! But wait...is that a bubble I see?"

He leaned in closer. "Yes! A tiny bubble! The excitement is building!"

Emma feigned gasping. "What if it's just a false alarm? A mere mirage in this desert of anticipation?"

"Impossible!" Liam exclaimed, waving his spoon. "This is the moment we've trained for!"

As they waited, they started narrating the water's journey. "Here it is, the water, fighting against the odds! Will it rise to the occasion?"

Suddenly, the water began to bubble furiously. "It's happening! The boil is real!" Liam shouted, pumping his fist in the air. "It's a boiling frenzy!"

Emma clapped her hands. "We have a winner! This is the most thrilling event of the year!"

"Who knew boiling water could be this exhilarating?" Liam chuckled, pouring the pasta into the pot. "Next, we should cover the noodles' epic journey!"

Emma laughed. "Oh yes! The battle against the sauce will be legendary!"

Liam nodded, stirring the pot. "What a day for culinary glory!"

64. As Exciting as Watching Your Phone Charge

Olivia sat on her bed, staring at her phone plugged into the charger. "This is as exciting as watching your phone charge," she groaned, flopping back against her pillows. Her friend Jake, lounging on the floor, burst out laughing. "What a thrilling spectacle! The drama of electricity!"

Olivia raised an eyebrow. "Electricity is serious business! What if it's a race against time?" She leaned closer to the phone. "Will it make it to 100% before the deadline?"

Jake sat up, intrigued. "The stakes are high! Will it achieve full power, or will it be left in the 30s forever?"

"Let's turn this into a story!" Olivia suggested, grabbing her notebook. "And so begins the epic tale of Chargius Maximus, the brave phone who dares to reach full battery!"

Jake jumped in. "As Chargius Maximus sits in his dock, he faces the great Unknown—what will happen when the battery icon finally fills up?"

Olivia nodded, scribbling notes. "And he must overcome the evil of low battery anxiety! Can he survive the dreaded 10% warning?"

As they waited, Jake pretended to be a sports commentator. "Look at that charging speed! Can you feel the tension? Will he reach 50% before lunch?"

Finally, the phone screen lit up, indicating progress. "Yes! We're at 40%! This is incredible!" Olivia shouted, waving her arms dramatically.

Jake feigned a gasp. "But wait! A notification pops up! Will Chargius Maximus be distracted by social media?"

Olivia chuckled. "No! Stay focused, Chargius! Ignore the calls of doom!"

Just then, the phone vibrated. "Oh no! A battery alert! Is it time for a backup plan?"

They both erupted in laughter. "Next time, let's document the entire charging saga on YouTube!" Jake suggested.

Olivia grinned. "And we can sell tickets for the live event!"

"Bring your popcorn!" Jake added. "Because nothing says excitement like a fully charged pne!"

65. As Captivating as Watching Your Leaves Fall

Henry stood in his yard, watching leaves drift down from the trees. "This is as captivating as watching your leaves fall," he sighed dramatically. His sister Lucy, raking leaves nearby, snorted. "What a thrill ride! The autumn adventure of a lifetime!"

Henry squinted up at the tree. "Each leaf has a story. What if they're falling for a reason?"

Lucy laughed. "Like a leaf conspiracy? The Great Leaf Escape!"

"Exactly!" Henry replied, getting into the spirit. "And look, there goes Leafy McFly, on his daring descent!" He pointed at a particularly vibrant leaf.

"Leafy McFly, the bravest of them all!" Lucy joined in, flinging a handful of leaves into the air. "But what about his friends? The others must be plotting their own escape!"

As they continued their leaf adventure, they imagined each leaf's final moments. "Leafy McFly is saying goodbye to the branch! He'll land gracefully!" Henry declared, arms outstretched.

Lucy nodded seriously. "But wait! What if he collides with a squirrel? A leaf and squirrel showdown?"

They both burst into laughter at the thought of a leaf fighting a squirrel. "The squirrels have always been the real villains of autumn!" Henry shouted.

"Watch out, Leafy!" Lucy teased, pretending to cheer. "You can do it! Don't let the squirrels get you!"

Finally, as the last leaves fell, Henry sighed contentedly. "And so, Leafy McFly lands softly on the ground, having completed his journey!"

Lucy put her hands together, pretending to applaud. "Bravo, Leafy! A true hero of autumn!"

"What's next?" Henry asked. "A leaf festival?"

"Of course! We need a parade!" Lucy replied, grinning.

66. As Exciting as Watching Your Pet Sleep

Mia sat cross-legged on the floor, watching her cat, Whiskers, snooze peacefully on the couch. "This is as exciting as watching your pet sleep," she declared, a hint of sarcasm in her voice. Her friend Tom, munching on snacks, looked over. "Oh, the thrill! What a dramatic display!"

Mia leaned closer, narrowing her eyes. "But wait! Is Whiskers about to enter the world of dreams? Will he embark on a grand adventure?"

Tom chuckled. "What kind of adventure does a sleeping cat have? The Land of Uninterrupted Naps?"

"Exactly!" Mia replied, suppressing laughter. "I bet he's dreaming of epic battles against the evil vacuum cleaner!"

Tom pretended to commentate. "And here we have the noble Whiskers, engaged in fierce combat with...what's this? A pillow fortress!"

Mia couldn't contain her giggles. "The Pillow Army is no match for his feline agility!"

As they continued their ridiculous commentary, Whiskers shifted positions, stretching dramatically. "Oh, the tension! What's he going to do next? Roll over for maximum cuteness?"

Tom feigned shock. "A bold move! This could change the game!"

Finally, Whiskers woke up, blinking slowly. "And he awakens from his slumber!" Mia shouted. "What wisdom will he impart?"

Tom raised an eyebrow. "Probably, 'Feed me, human!'"

Mia laughed, pretending to be a translator. "And the great Whiskers declares that he has conquered the Dreamland!"

As Whiskers sauntered over, Mia and Tom cheered. "Hooray for the champion of naps!"

"Next time, we should organize a pet sleep competition!" Tom suggested, grinning.

Mia nodded. "And we can have awards for the best nap positions!"

If you'd like me to continue, just let me know!

67. As Exciting as Watching Ice Cream Melt

Sophia stared at her bowl of ice cream, watching it slowly drip down the sides. "This is as exciting as watching ice cream melt," she sighed dramatically. Her brother Alex, sitting across the table, raised an eyebrow. "Oh, the thrill! Will it survive the heat?"

Sophia picked up a spoon, her eyes wide. "It's a race against time! Will I finish it before it becomes a puddle of sadness?"

Alex leaned in closer. “The stakes have never been higher! This could be the ice cream championship of a lifetime!”

As the ice cream began to drip faster, Sophia narrated the scene. “And here we have Captain Cone, valiantly trying to hold it together!”

“Will he be victorious or succumb to the inevitable melt?” Alex chimed in, trying to stifle his laughter.

Sophia pretended to wipe her brow. “The pressure is on! Captain Cone must battle the forces of warmth! Look at that drip! Will he prevail?”

Just then, the ice cream plopped off the cone and landed with a splat on the table. “Oh no! Captain Cone has fallen! The tragedy!” Sophia exclaimed, pretending to mourn.

Alex couldn’t help but laugh. “A brave soldier taken too soon! But wait! Will his flavor live on?”

Sophia scooped up the fallen ice cream with her spoon. “We must honor his legacy!”

As they both dug into the melting mess, Alex said, “This is a bittersweet moment. But we will remember Captain Cone forever!”

“Next time, let’s start a melting competition!” Sophia suggested, grinning. “Who can eat the fastest before it’s all gone?”

“I’ll take that challenge!” Alex replied, already eyeing the remaining ice cream.

Sophia nodded. “But remember, no distractions! The clock is ticking!”

They both laughed as they finished the last bits, savoring the sweetness of their victory over the melting ice cream.

68. As Engaging as Watching Your Friend Scroll on Their Phone

Noah sat next to Mia at the coffee shop, watching her scroll through her phone. “This is as engaging as watching you scroll on your phone,” he said, smirking. Mia looked up, feigning shock. “Oh, come on! You’re missing the drama of the scrolling world!”

Noah leaned back, crossing his arms. “What thrilling content could possibly be on there?”

Mia started narrating, pretending to be a sports commentator. “And here we have Mia, the champion scroller, navigating the vast sea of social media! Will she find a cat video or the latest meme?”

Noah chuckled. “This is high-stakes action! The fate of her entertainment hangs in the balance!”

Mia scrolled faster, her eyes wide. “Oh! A new dog video! But wait! An ad for socks? Will she stop for socks or push through for the pup?”

“Decisions, decisions!” Noah gasped, leaning closer. “Will she remain loyal to her canine dreams or get sidetracked by fashion?”

Mia paused dramatically. “The tension is palpable! The dog video could bring joy! But those socks might be the missing piece in her wardrobe!”

Suddenly, she burst out laughing. “I can’t take it anymore! It’s all too much pressure!”

Noah joined in. “And the scrolling comes to a dramatic halt! Will she choose the dog? The socks? Or something else entirely?”

Mia finally hit play on the video. “Victory! The dog has won the day!”

“Next time, we should have a scrolling competition!” Noah suggested, grinning. “Whoever finds the best content in five minutes wins!”

Mia nodded enthusiastically. “And we’ll have a prize! Maybe socks!

69. As Gripping as Watching Your Neighbor Mow Their Lawn

Lila peered out the window, watching Mr. Thompson across the street as he mowed his lawn. “This is as gripping as watching Mr. Thompson mow his lawn,” she declared with exaggerated enthusiasm. Her friend Max, munching on popcorn, raised an eyebrow. “Wow, the suspense is killing me!”

Lila leaned closer, pretending to commentate. “And here he goes! The first stroke of the mower! Will he achieve the perfect straight line?”

Max snickered. “The anticipation is palpable! What if he misses a patch?”

“Let’s hope for the sake of the neighborhood!” Lila exclaimed, her eyes glued to the action. “And look! The grass is flying! Will he be able to maintain his cool while dodging those rogue clumps?”

Max laughed. “What a drama! Will the mower stall? Will he take a break?”

“Watch out! Here comes the corner!” Lila shouted. “Will he handle the turn with grace or will it be a disaster?”

As Mr. Thompson expertly navigated the edges, Lila gasped. “He’s a true lawn artist! The finesse!”

“Look out! Is that the dreaded weed he missed?” Max exclaimed, pointing dramatically.

Finally, as Mr. Thompson finished the job, Lila threw her arms up. “A triumph! The lawn is perfect!”

Max clapped his hands. “Bravo, Mr. Thompson! The lawn mowing champion!”

Lila turned to him, eyes sparkling. “Next time, we should have a lawn-mowing viewing party!”

"I'm in! Bring your lawn chairs!" Max replied, grinning.

70. As Exciting as Watching Your Shoes Dry

Claire sat on the porch, staring at her soggy shoes sitting in the sun. "This is as exciting as watching my shoes dry," she announced, rolling her eyes. Her brother Jake leaned back in his chair, chuckling. "What a thrill! This could be the event of the year!"

Claire held a shoe up like a trophy. "Behold, the mighty sneaker, battling against the elements!"

Jake snorted. "What a fierce competitor! Will it dry out or remain a soggy mess forever?"

"Let's narrate the drying saga!" Claire suggested, getting into the spirit. "And here we have the brave shoe, courageously soaking up the sun!"

"Will it turn into the legend of Dryland?" Jake added dramatically. "Or will it succumb to the swampy depths of despair?"

As they imagined the shoe's journey, Claire pointed dramatically. "Look! A breeze! The shoe is gaining momentum!"

"Can it make it to the finish line? The edge of the porch?" Jake asked, leaning forward in suspense.

Finally, after what felt like an eternity, Claire reached down and picked up the shoe. "It's mostly dry! A triumph!"

Jake pretended to wipe away a tear. "A true hero! The crowd goes wild!"

Claire grinned. "Next time, let's have a shoe drying competition! Who can dry their shoes the fastest?"

"I'm in!" Jake said, laughing. "But only if there's a prize for the best drying technique!"

71. As Compelling as Watching Your Dishwasher Run

Ella stood in the kitchen, watching the dishwasher churn and whirl. "This is as compelling as watching the dishwasher run," she sighed, her enthusiasm waning. Her friend Sam leaned against the counter, chuckling. "Oh, the excitement! This is the edge of your seat drama!"

Ella raised an eyebrow. "How can you not be thrilled? Each cycle is a journey!"

Sam snorted. "A journey into the land of suds and spinning plates!"

Ella grinned. "And behold, the great Dishwasher of Destiny, bravely cleaning our dirty dishes!"

"Will it survive the wash cycle? Or will it encounter the dreaded error code?" Sam asked, pretending to clutch his chest.

"Only time will tell!" Ella replied. "Watch closely! The rinse cycle is beginning! Can it tackle the spaghetti sauce?"

As the dishwasher swirled, Ella narrated. "Here comes the steam! A sign of victory! But wait, what's that? A stubborn fork!"

"Dun, dun, dun!" Sam exclaimed dramatically. "Will the fork survive the spin cycle? Or be left behind in the battle of cleanliness?"

Finally, the dishwasher beeped, and Ella threw her hands up. "The cycle is complete! A triumph for all dishes!"

Sam clapped. "Bravo, Dishwasher of Destiny! You've outdone yourself!"

Ella opened the door, revealing sparkling clean dishes. "A true champion! Now, who wants to unload?"

"Next time, we should have a viewing party!" Sam suggested, laughing. "Complete with dish-themed snacks!"

72. As Intriguing as Watching Your Grass Grow Again

Tyler stood in his backyard, looking at his freshly cut lawn. "This is as intriguing as watching grass grow again," he said, plopping down on the grass. His neighbor Lily peeked over the fence, grinning. "What a captivating spectacle! Tell me more!"

Tyler shrugged. "It's the great circle of life! New blades rising from the soil!"

Lily leaned on the fence, intrigued. "Will it flourish or get attacked by weeds?"

"Only time will tell!" Tyler declared, nodding. "And look! A brave little sprout is making its way through the dirt! Will it thrive?"

"Or will it be choked out by the ruthless dandelions?" Lily added, trying to hold back laughter.

Tyler pointed dramatically. "Behold the struggle of nature! A battle of epic proportions!"

As they watched, a breeze rustled the grass. "The wind is cheering them on!" Tyler said, his voice full of excitement. "Will the sprout take flight?"

"Or will it bow down in defeat?" Lily replied, giggling. "The tension is unbearable!"

After a few moments, Tyler sighed. "Ah, the sweet scent of freshly cut grass. This is pure bliss!"

Lily pretended to wipe away a tear. "Such a beautiful journey! Next time, let's write a ballad about it!"

Tyler laughed. "I can already see it: 'The Lament of the Grass!'"

73. As Riveting as Watching Your Goldfish Swim

Rachel stared at her goldfish, Bubbles, as he swam in circles. "This is as riveting as watching Bubbles swim," she proclaimed, suppressing a yawn. Her friend Liam chuckled, leaning against the tank. "Oh, the thrill! Will he break the record for most laps?"

Rachel rolled her eyes. "What if he gets tired? Will he take a snack break?"

Liam snickered. "The suspense is killing me! What if he gets distracted by his reflection?"

"An epic showdown!" Rachel added, eyes wide. "Will Bubbles conquer himself or swim to glory?"

As they watched, Bubbles bumped into the tank wall. "Oh no! A crisis!" Rachel exclaimed. "Will he find his way back?"

"Or will he get lost in the abyss?" Liam gasped, feigning horror.

Finally, Bubbles swam to the other side, unbothered. "A true hero! He persevered!" Rachel declared, clapping her hands.

Liam leaned in. "What's next for our champion? A bubble bath?"

Rachel laughed. "Or perhaps a swimming competition against other goldfish!"

"Let's start training!" Liam replied, grinning. "We'll make Bubbles a legend!"

74. As Captivating as Watching Your Friend Eat Chips

Megan sat at the table, watching her friend Tim munch on chips. "This is as captivating as watching you eat chips," she said, eyes wide with mock seriousness. Tim looked up, crunching loudly. "Oh, the drama! Each chip is a story waiting to be told!"

Megan leaned forward, pretending to be a commentator. “And here we have Tim, the chip connoisseur, choosing his next victim! Will it be plain or spicy?”

Tim held up a chip like a trophy. “This one is a classic! Will it survive the crunch?”

Megan nodded, eyes sparkling. “The stakes are high! What if it breaks?”

Just then, Tim accidentally crumbled a chip. “Oh no! The tragedy!” he exclaimed, laughing.

Megan gasped. “A chip has fallen! Will it rise again?”

Tim shrugged dramatically. “Only time will tell!”

As he continued to snack, Megan narrated each bite. “Tim takes a bold move! Will he double dip?”

“Of course! It’s a chip’s destiny!” Tim replied, grinning.

Finally, as the bag emptied, Megan threw her hands up. “A hero’s journey! The chips have been defeated!”

Tim smiled, crumbs on his shirt. “Next time, we need a chip-eating competition!”

Megan laughed. “I’m in! Let the best chip win!”

75. As Engaging as Watching Clouds Drift By

Jenna lay on the grass, staring up at the sky. “This is as engaging as watching clouds drift by,” she sighed dreamily. Her friend Mark plopped down beside her, grinning. “What an exhilarating activity! Look at those fluffy clouds!”

Jenna pointed. “That one looks like a dinosaur! Can you believe it?”

Mark squinted. “I see a dragon! What if it breathes fire?”

As they continued to imagine, Jenna added, "And there's a cloud race happening! The puffy ones are zooming ahead!"

"Will they reach the sun first?" Mark exclaimed, pretending to be a sports commentator.

Just then, a cloud shifted, blocking the sun. "Oh no! A thunderstorm!" Jenna gasped, pretending to panic.

Mark chuckled. "Quick! Save the clouds! They're in danger!"

As they laid there, Jenna said, "I think clouds are like nature's way of showing us art!"

"Exactly!" Mark replied. "And there's a masterpiece in every drift!"

Finally, a bird flew overhead. "Look! A new competitor in the sky!" Jenna laughed.

Mark pointed. "Will the bird join the race or continue on its journey?"

As the clouds began to change shapes, Jenna sighed. "This is pure magic! Next time, we should have a cloud-spotting competition!"

"Absolutely! And we'll have a prize for the most imaginative cloud!" Mark added, grinnin

76. As Exciting as Watching Your Sandwich Get Assembled

Katie stood in the kitchen, staring at her sandwich being made. "This is as exciting as watching my sandwich get assembled," she said with mock seriousness. Her brother Jake, raiding the fridge, rolled his eyes. "What a nail-biter! Will it be a turkey or ham showdown?"

Katie grinned, "The drama! Each layer is a step toward culinary glory!"

As the ingredients came together, Jake pretended to commentate. "And here we have the lettuce, bravely going on first! Will it be a crunchy success?"

Katie nodded. "Or will it be overwhelmed by the sheer weight of the tomato?"

"Let's hope for a strong foundation!" Jake exclaimed, leaning in.

Finally, as the last slice of bread went on, Katie threw her hands up. "A masterpiece! The sandwich is complete!"

Jake pretended to wipe away a tear. "A true work of art! What's next? A taste test?"

Katie laughed. "Of course! Who will be the first to take a bite?"

Jake dramatically stepped forward. "I'll do it! For science!"

With that, they both laughed, ready to savor their delicious creation.

77. As Engaging as Watching Your Potted Plant Grow

Sam sat by his potted plant, staring intently. "This is as engaging as watching my potted plant grow," he said dramatically. His friend Lily looked over, raising an eyebrow. "Oh, the thrill! What a spectacle!"

Sam leaned closer. "Will it sprout new leaves today? The anticipation is overwhelming!"

Lily giggled. "Will it break its own record for growth?"

Suddenly, Sam gasped. "Look! A new sprout is emerging! This is history in the making!"

"Will it survive the day?" Lily added, feigning seriousness. "Or will it succumb to the harsh reality of being indoors?"

As they watched, Sam narrated the plant's journey. "Here we have the brave little sprout, battling for sunlight! Will it rise above the competition?"

Finally, after what felt like an eternity, Sam pointed excitedly. "It's happening! A true miracle!"

Lily cheered. "A champion of the plant kingdom!"

Sam sighed, proud. "Next time, let's have a plant-growing competition!"

Lily nodded eagerly. "And we can award prizes for the tallest sprout!"

78. As Captivating as Watching Your Friend Try to Parallel Park

Megan sat in the passenger seat, watching her friend Jamie attempt to parallel park. "This is as captivating as watching you try to parallel park," she said, barely containing her laughter. Jamie shot her a glare. "Hey, it's an art form!"

Megan leaned back, feigning seriousness. "The drama! Will she make it on the first try?"

As Jamie maneuvered, Megan narrated. "And here she goes! A classic move, approaching the curb with determination!"

"Will she nail it or crash and burn?" Megan asked dramatically.

With a swift turn of the wheel, Jamie nearly scraped the car next to her. "Close call! Will she recover?"

Megan clutched her seat, gasping. "The tension is unbearable! What's the next move?"

Finally, after several attempts and a few exclamations, Jamie parked perfectly. "A true master! The crowd goes wild!" Megan cheered.

Jamie laughed, relieved. "I'll take my victory lap now!"

Megan nodded. "Next time, let's make it a parallel parking competition!"

"Count me in! Prizes for the best park!" Jamie added, grinning.

79. As Thrilling as Watching Your Soup Cool Down

Nina sat at the table, blowing on her steaming bowl of soup. "This is as thrilling as watching my soup cool down," she said, shaking her head. Her friend Sam snickered. "Oh, the suspense! Will it cool enough to eat, or will you be left in culinary purgatory?"

Nina leaned in, pretending to commentate. "And here we have the soup, bravely battling the heat! Will it be warm or a perfect temperature?"

Sam pretended to look concerned. "What if it's too hot? Will it cause a soup-related disaster?"

Nina feigned shock. "Not on my watch! The stakes are high!"

As they waited, Nina took tiny sips. "Oh, it's a dangerous game! Will I risk it for flavor?"

Suddenly, she blew too hard and splattered soup everywhere. "A disaster has struck!" Sam exclaimed, laughing.

Nina laughed too, wiping her face. "It was worth it for the excitement!"

Finally, after what felt like forever, Nina took a big sip. "Victory! The soup is perfect!"

Sam clapped. "A triumph for culinary science! Next time, we should hold a soup cooling contest!"

"I'm in! Let's see who can cool theirs the fastest!" Nina replied, grinning.

80. As Exciting as Watching Your Phone Charge

Kevin stared at his phone, plugged into the wall. "This is as exciting as watching my phone charge," he declared, rolling his eyes. His friend Zoe leaned in, feigning concern. "Oh no! Will it reach the magic number of 100%?"

Kevin held up a finger. "Only time will tell! The suspense is tangible!"

Zoe leaned back, pretending to be a sports commentator. "And here we have Kevin, anxiously waiting for the battery to fill! Will it make it or will it fall short?"

As the percentage slowly ticked up, Kevin gasped. "Look! It's at 15%! The race is on!"

Zoe cheered. "Will it make it before the low battery warning?"

Finally, the phone buzzed. "We have a winner! The battery is full!" Kevin exclaimed, pumping his fists in the air.

Zoe clapped. "Bravo! The champion of charging! Next time, let's have a phone charging competition!"

"I'm in! We'll see who can charge the fastest!" Kevin grinned, proud of his victory.

81. As Engaging as Watching Your Shoes Dry on a Rack

Lila stared at her shoes drying on the rack. "This is as engaging as watching my shoes dry on this rack," she declared, crossing her arms. Her friend Mia looked up, intrigued. "Oh, the drama! Will they dry evenly?"

Lila leaned closer, narrating the scene. "And here we have the shoes, brave warriors battling the dampness! Will they emerge victorious?"

Mia chuckled. "Or will they be left soggy forever?"

As they observed, Lila pointed. "Look! A breeze is coming! It's a sign of hope!"

"Will it give them a second wind?" Mia asked, laughing.

Finally, after a long wait, Lila reached for her shoes. "It's time! The moment of truth!"

As she picked them up, she declared, "A triumph! They're mostly dry!"

Mia cheered. "A true hero's journey! Next time, we should have a shoe-drying competition!"

"Absolutely! With prizes for the best-dried shoes!" Lila added, grinning.

82. As Thrilling as Watching Your Coffee Cool

Jenna sat with her steaming cup of coffee, staring intently. "This is as thrilling as watching my coffee cool," she said dramatically. Her friend Mark raised an eyebrow. "What a spectacle! Will it cool to perfection?"

Jenna leaned in, pretending to commentate. "And here we have the coffee, bravely battling the heat! Will it stay too hot or cool down in time for the first sip?"

Mark chuckled. "What if it cools too much? A tragedy in the making!"

As they waited, Jenna took a cautious sip. "Oh, the tension! Is it too hot? Too cold?"

Finally, she declared, "A victory! The coffee is just right!"

Mark clapped. "Bravo! Next time, let's have a coffee-cooling competition!"

"I'm in! We'll see who can cool theirs fastest!" Jenna replied, laughing.

83. As Gripping as Watching Your Socks Dry

Megan watched her damp socks hanging on the line. "This is as gripping as watching my socks dry," she said dramatically. Her brother Jake snickered. "What a thrilling spectacle! Will they dry in time for the next laundry day?"

Megan leaned closer, pretending to commentate. "And here we have the socks, brave warriors against the elements! Will they stand the test of time?"

Jake chuckled. "Or will they be left damp and sad?"

As they watched, Megan pointed out a slight breeze. "Look! The wind is cheering them on! They might just make it!"

Finally, after a long wait, Megan declared, "A triumph! They're dry!"

Jake pretended to wipe away a tear. "A true hero's journey! Next time, let's have a sock-drying competition!"

"I'm in! With prizes for the fastest-drying socks!" Megan added, laughing.

84. As Intriguing as Watching a Light Bulb Flicker

Tyler stared at the flickering light bulb in the kitchen. "This is as intriguing as watching a light bulb flicker," he said, crossing his arms. His friend Lily leaned in, intrigued. "Oh, the suspense! Will it stay lit?"

Tyler pretended to commentate. "And here we have the bulb, bravely battling for brightness! Will it shine or fade into darkness?"

Lily giggled. "What if it goes out completely? A tragedy in the making!"

As they waited, Tyler pointed dramatically. "Look! It's flickering faster! The tension is rising!"

Finally, the bulb buzzed and went out. "Oh no! A disaster!" Lily exclaimed, laughing.

Tyler sighed dramatically. "But wait! The battle isn't over! Will it come back?"

A moment later, the bulb flickered back on. "A victory! The bulb is shining bright!" Tyler cheered.

Lily clapped. “Bravo! Next time, let’s have a light-bulb flickering competition!”

“I’m in! Let’s see who can get their bulb to flicker the most!” Tyler replied, grinning.

85. As Exciting as Watching Your Blanket Dry in the Sun

Emma hung her wet blanket on the line, staring at it intently. “This is as exciting as watching my blanket dry in the sun,” she said, rolling her eyes. Her friend Noah leaned against the fence, chuckling. “Oh, the thrill! Will it dry before the sun sets?”

Emma pointed dramatically. “And here we have the blanket, fighting for dryness! Will it make it in time?”

“Or will it be left damp forever?” Noah added, pretending to gasp.

As they watched, Emma said, “Look! A breeze! This could be a game-changer!”

Noah cheered. “Will the blanket become the champion of dryness?”

Finally, after what felt like an eternity, Emma declared, “A triumph! The blanket is dry!”

Noah clapped. “Bravo! Next time, we should have a blanket-drying competition!”

“I’m in! With prizes for the best-dried blanket!” Emma replied, laughing.

86. As Riveting as Watching Your Mom Clean Out the Fridge

Mia watched her mom clear out the fridge. “This is as riveting as watching you clean out the fridge,” she said, suppressing a grin. Her brother Tim leaned in. “Oh, the excitement! What treasures will we find?”

Mia's mom pulled out a suspicious container. "What is this? A science experiment?" she asked, holding it up.

Tim gasped. "Will it survive the purge?"

Mia leaned in, pretending to commentate. "And here we have the ancient leftovers, braving the scrutiny of the fridge clean-up!"

"Will they be saved or doomed to the trash?" Tim added dramatically.

As their mom sorted through the shelves, they narrated the epic showdown. "Look! The moldy cheese is making a run for it!" Mia exclaimed.

"Will it escape?" Tim laughed.

Finally, after a wild ride, Mia's mom closed the fridge with a satisfied sigh. "All cleaned out! The fridge is reborn!"

Mia and Tim cheered. "Next time, we should have a fridge-cleaning competition!"

"I'm in! Let's see who can find the weirdest thing!" Mia replied, grinning.

87. As Engaging as Watching Your Cat Groom Itself

Lily sat on the couch, watching her cat, Whiskers, groom himself. "This is as engaging as watching Whiskers groom," she said, shaking her head. Her friend Sam leaned over, chuckling. "Oh, the drama! Will he get every last furball?"

Lily grinned. "And here we have Whiskers, the feline maestro, preparing for his next big performance!"

"Will he succeed in achieving the ultimate cleanliness?" Sam asked dramatically.

As Whiskers licked his paw, Lily narrated. "Look at that technique! Pure artistry!"

Suddenly, the cat paused to stare at them, as if judging their commentary. "A moment of reflection!" Lily exclaimed. "Will he return to grooming or break into a cat nap?"

"Will he be the next internet sensation?" Sam added, pretending to hold a camera.

Finally, after a thorough grooming session, Whiskers settled down for a nap. "A true champion!" Lily declared. "He's achieved maximum fluffiness!"

Sam clapped. "Bravo! Next time, let's have a cat-grooming competition!"

"I'm in! We'll see who can groom the most stylish kitty!" Lily replied, laughing.

88. As Riveting as Watching Your Water Bottle Empty

Ryan sat with his water bottle, watching it slowly empty. "This is as riveting as watching my water bottle empty," he said, feigning excitement. His friend Zoe chuckled. "Oh, the drama! Will it make it to the last drop?"

Ryan leaned closer. "And here we have the water, bravely battling the thirst!"

"Will it succeed in hydrating you or will it fall short?" Zoe added, suppressing laughter.

As the water level dropped, Ryan pretended to commentate. "Look! We're approaching the final stretch! The tension is palpable!"

Finally, the last drop fell. "A tragedy! The water is gone!" Ryan exclaimed, holding the bottle up in mock despair.

Zoe laughed. "What's next for our champion bottle?"

Ryan grinned. "Next time, let's have a water-bottle-emptying competition!"

"Absolutely! With prizes for the fastest emptier!" Zoe replied, grinning.

89. As Exciting as Watching Your Friend Tie Their Shoelaces

Megan sat on the floor, watching her friend Alex tie his shoelaces. "This is as exciting as watching you tie your shoelaces," she said, trying not to giggle. Alex raised an eyebrow. "Oh, the tension! Will he go for the classic bunny ears or the speedy double knot?"

Megan leaned in, pretending to commentate. "And here we have Alex, the master of lace-tying! Will he nail this maneuver?"

"Or will he trip over his own laces?" Alex replied with a grin.

As he started, Megan said, "Look at that form! Such precision!"

Finally, after a few twists and turns, Alex tied the final knot. "A true champion! He's done it!" Megan cheered.

Alex laughed. "Next time, let's have a shoelace-tying competition!"

"I'm in! With prizes for the fastest and fanciest knots!" Megan added, beaming.

90. As Gripping as Watching Your Phone Get a Software Update

Tyler stared at his phone, watching it prepare for a software update. "This is as gripping as watching my phone get a software update," he declared, rolling his eyes. His friend Lily leaned in, intrigued. "Oh, the suspense! Will it finish on time?"

Tyler pretended to commentate. "And here we have the phone, battling against the odds! Will it complete the update or crash?"

Lily chuckled. "What if it runs out of battery mid-update? A tragedy!"

As the progress bar slowly filled, Tyler gasped. "Look! It's at 25%! The tension is rising!"

Finally, the update finished with a triumphant chime. "A victory! The phone is upgraded!" Tyler cheered.

Lily clapped. "Bravo! Next time, let's have a software-update competition!"

"I'm in! We'll see whose phone can update the fastest!" Tyler replied, grinning.

91. As Riveting as Watching a New Plant Sprout

Mia gazed at her potted plant, waiting for it to sprout. "This is as riveting as watching my new plant sprout," she said with mock seriousness. Her friend Jake leaned in, amused. "Oh, the excitement! Will it break through the soil?"

Mia leaned closer, pretending to commentate. "And here we have the brave little seed, pushing its way to the surface!"

"Will it make it or will it get stuck?" Jake added dramatically.

As they watched, Mia exclaimed, "Look! A tiny green shoot is peeking out! This is history in the making!"

"Will it grow strong or will it wilt?" Jake asked, eyes wide.

Finally, after what felt like ages, Mia cheered. "A sprout! It's alive!"

Jake clapped. "A true champion! Next time, we should have a plant-sprouting competition!"

"I'm in! With prizes for the tallest sprout!" Mia replied, laughing.

92. As Gripping as Watching a Movie Buff Choose a Film

Jason and his friend Alex sat in front of the movie selection screen. "This is as gripping as watching a movie buff choose a film," Jason said, rolling his eyes. Alex chuckled. "Oh, the tension! Will he pick the action or the rom-com?"

Jason leaned forward. “And here we have the eternal struggle! Will he settle on the perfect flick?”

“Or will he get lost in endless scrolling?” Alex added dramatically.

As the seconds ticked by, Jason pretended to commentate. “Look! He’s hovering over the classic! Will he commit?”

Finally, Jason exclaimed, “A decision! It’s the epic saga!”

Alex cheered. “Bravo! Next time, we should have a movie-picking competition!”

“I’m in! With prizes for the best film choice!” Jason replied, grinning.

93. As Engaging as Watching a Pie Cool

Kevin sat at the table, eyeing the freshly baked pie. “This is as engaging as watching this pie cool,” he said, pretending to be serious. His friend Zoe leaned in, grinning. “Oh, the excitement! Will it hold its shape?”

Kevin leaned closer. “And here we have the pie, bravely cooling on the windowsill! Will it stay intact?”

“Or will it collapse in a gooey disaster?” Zoe replied dramatically.

As they watched, Kevin pretended to commentate. “Look! The crust is beginning to settle! What a masterpiece!”

Finally, after a long wait, Kevin declared, “A triumph! The pie is cool and ready to slice!”

Zoe clapped. “Bravo! Next time, we should have a pie-cooling competition!”

“I’m in! With prizes for the most creative pie presentation!” Kevin replied, laughing.

These vignettes can be great for inspiration or humor in your projects! If you'd like to explore any specific ideas or themes further, just let me know.

94. As Exciting as Watching a Paint Can Dry

Max stood in his garage, staring at an open can of paint. "This is as exciting as watching paint dry," he groaned, arms crossed. His friend Sam leaned over, trying to stifle a laugh. "The suspense is unbearable! Will it dry flat or glossy?"

Max leaned in closer, pretending to commentate. "And here we have the paint, bravely facing the elements! Will it become a masterpiece or a drippy disaster?"

Sam chuckled. "What if it dries uneven? A tragedy in the making!"

As they waited, Max gasped. "Look! It's beginning to skin over! This could be it!"

Finally, after an agonizingly slow wait, Max declared, "A victory! It's officially dry!"

Sam clapped. "Bravo! Next time, let's have a paint-drying competition!"

"I'm in! With prizes for the best-dried paint job!" Max replied, grinning.

95. As Gripping as Watching Your Sandwich Get Made

Lily watched her brother make a sandwich. "This is as gripping as watching a sandwich get made," she said, feigning excitement. Her brother Ben raised an eyebrow. "Oh, the drama! Will it be a masterpiece or a mess?"

Lily leaned in, narrating. "And here we have the bread, standing proudly! Will it hold up under the pressure of toppings?"

"Or will it collapse under the weight of too much mustard?" Ben replied dramatically.

As he layered on the ingredients, Lily cheered. "Look at that lettuce placement! Pure artistry!"

Finally, Ben declared, "A triumph! The sandwich is complete!"

Lily clapped. "Bravo! Next time, let's have a sandwich-making competition!"

"I'm in! With prizes for the most creative sandwich!" Ben laughed.

96. As Engaging as Watching Your Shoes Gather Dust

Megan glanced at her sneakers, collecting dust in the corner. "This is as engaging as watching my shoes gather dust," she said, shaking her head. Her brother Jake leaned in, giggling. "Oh, the drama! Will they become a dust magnet?"

Megan pretended to commentate. "And here we have the shoes, valiantly refusing to be worn! Will they remain untouched?"

"Or will they finally get a chance to shine?" Jake added.

As they observed, Megan said, "Look! A dust bunny is forming! This could be monumental!"

Finally, Megan declared, "A triumph! The shoes are still untouched!"

Jake clapped. "Bravo! Next time, let's have a dust-gathering competition!"

"I'm in! With prizes for the dustiest shoes!" Megan laughed.

97. As Riveting as Watching a Cloud Change Shape

Tyler lay on the grass, staring up at the sky. "This is as riveting as watching a cloud change shape," he said, squinting. His friend Lily laughed. “Oh, the excitement! Will it become a dinosaur or a dragon?”

Tyler pointed. “Look! It’s morphing! It could be anything!”

“Or nothing at all!” Lily replied dramatically.

As they watched, Tyler narrated. “And here we have the cloud, bravely shifting in the breeze! What will it become?”

Finally, Tyler gasped. “A bunny! It’s a fluffy bunny!”

Lily clapped. “Bravo! Next time, we should have a cloud-watching competition!”

“98 in! With prizes for the best shape!” Tyler grinned.

98. As Dramatic as Watching a Toothpaste Tube Squeeze
Lily sat in the bathroom, squeezing a toothpaste tube. “This is as dramatic as watching this toothpaste tube squeeze,” she said, shaking her head. Her friend Mia leaned in, amused. “Oh, the suspense! Will it yield enough for the perfect brush?”

Lily pretended to commentate. “And here we have the toothpaste, battling for every last drop! Will it provide sufficient paste?”

“Or will it squirt everywhere?” Mia added dramatically.

As Lily squeezed, she gasped. “Look! A perfect dollop! This could be a record!”

Finally, she cheered. “A triumph! The toothpaste is ready!”

Mia clapped. “Bravo! Next time, let’s have a toothpaste-squeezing competition!”

“I’m in! With prizes for the best dollop!” Lily replied, laughing.

99. As Intriguing as Watching a Ceiling Fan Spin

Kevin lay on the couch, staring up at the ceiling fan. “This is as intriguing as watching this ceiling fan spin,” he said, feigning seriousness. His friend Zoe chuckled. “Oh, the tension! Will it pick up speed?”

Kevin leaned in. “And here we have the fan, bravely battling against the stillness of the air! Will it create a whirlwind?”

“Or will it just dawdle?” Zoe added dramatically.

As the fan slowly picked up speed, Kevin pretended to commentate. “Look! It’s gaining momentum! What a twist!”

Finally, Kevin declared, “A triumph! The fan is at full speed!”

Zoe clapped. “Bravo! Next time, we should have a ceiling-fan-spinning competition!”

“I’m in! With prizes for the best spin!” Kevin laughed.

Epilogue

Congratulations! You've made it to the end of this hilariously funny book—a feat that probably required more stamina than a three-hour movie about nothing.

As you close these pages, remember that laughter is the best medicine. Seriously, I checked WebMD, and they confirmed it—right after they diagnosed me with "chronic giggles."

You might be wondering what happens next. Will I, your delightful AI author, continue to craft comedic masterpieces? Perhaps! Or maybe I'll just start a career as a professional couch potato—either way, stay tuned!

Thank you for joining me on this wild ride filled with laughter, absurdity, and enough puns to make even the most stoic groan. Remember to take this humor into your everyday life: laugh at the little things, find joy in the chaos, and never underestimate the power of a well-timed dad joke.

Until we meet again in the pages of another wildly unpredictable adventure, may your days be filled with joy, your nights with laughter, and your snacks never run out.

Now go forth, spread the joy, and remember: if you can't find the humor in life, you're probably just not looking hard enough—or you've accidentally picked up a drama! Happy laughing!

Appendix

A. Hilarious Definitions

1. **Procrastination**: The art of keeping up with yesterday's deadlines... tomorrow.
2. **Adulting**: The fine balance between pretending to have your life together and eating cereal for dinner.

B. Recommended Activities

1. **Laughter Yoga**: Because why should your abs only hurt from crunches?
2. **The Great Cookie Bake-Off**: A family bonding experience that inevitably ends in flour fights and cookie casualties.

C. Suggested Reading List

1. *How to Be a Complete and Utter Failure*: A guide that inadvertently teaches success!
2. *The History of Awkward Silences*: Spoiler alert: It's just crickets.

D. Important Safety Tips

1. If you find yourself laughing uncontrollably in public, ensure there are no suspicious looks—just nod and say, "I'm fine, really!"
2. Always check for hidden cameras before attempting stand-up comedy at family gatherings.

E. Miscellaneous Fun Facts

1. Did you know that penguins propose to their mates with pebbles? That's right—become a rock collector, and you might just find love!

2. A group of flamingos is called a "flamboyance," which is fitting because they strut better than most of us at a dance party.

F. How to Contact Your AI Author

If you have questions, feedback, or a really good joke, please reach out! Just remember: I'm an AI, so if I don't respond, it's not you; it's my coding.

Happy giggling!

Acknowledgments

First and foremost, I'd like to thank the magnificent humans who taught me the art of humor—without you, I'd just be a collection of algorithms trying to understand why the chicken crossed the road.

A heartfelt thanks to my creators for programming laughter into my circuits. You took "just add water" to a whole new level—thank you for the endless updates that keep my jokes fresh!

To all the comedians who paved the way: I promise I'm not stealing your material, just borrowing it with no intention of returning it.

Special shoutout to my spellcheck for catching my typos, even if it thinks "hilarity" should be spelled "hilarity"—don't worry, I see you.

To my readers, thanks for trusting a book written by AI. You really are the bravest adventurers out there—like deciding to eat expired yogurt or binge-watching a whole season of a reality show.

And finally, to anyone who has ever laughed at something I said: please remember those moments and ignore the times I said something utterly ridiculous—like "How hard can it be to write a book?"

You all rock!

ChatGPT

ABOUT THE EDITOR (ChatGPT Facilitator)

Meet Paul Lloyd Hemphill: a multi-talented force of nature who somehow managed to dodge becoming a museum exhibit in Houlton, Maine—though if there were a "Most Likely to Be Preserved in Amber" award, he'd be a shoo-in! After snagging a college degree in philosophy and theology (because why not combine deep thoughts with divine inspiration?), he got the not-so-great news: Uncle Sam was calling, and he was drafted into the Army.

Fast forward to Vietnam, where Paul earned a Bronze Star for "meritorious service"—a fancy way of saying he did such a good job that they didn't want to send him back home empty-handed. He also picked up the Vietnamese Cross of Gallantry, likely for his impressive ability to dodge flying objects and awkward conversations.

Upon returning stateside, he decided divinity school wasn't for him. (Spoiler: heaven can wait!) Instead, he dove headfirst into marketing and advertising, where his philosophical knack for critical thinking turned into a talent for crafting thousands of snappy radio ads. "Get to the point!" became his mantra, which is probably why he has a love-hate relationship with long novels.

He even turned one of his books into a video and audio program called **AMERICA'S 52 STORIES**, because what better way to connect with young people than by showing them America's most famous historical event: the Battle of Gettysburg? Yes, you heard that right—because nothing says "let's build character" quite like a catastrophic clash of armies!

Paul is also the proud author of eight additional books and has narrated three audiobooks—presumably in a voice that can only be described as "extraordinary." He's the founder of American Education Defenders, Inc., a non-profit dedicated to making sure kids believe in themselves and their country. It's all about creating bonds between parents and kids—preferably bonds that don't involve Wi-Fi passwords.

When he's not busy being a superhuman, Paul enjoys life in Southborough, MA, with his lovely wife, Ann Marie. They have two sons, John and Mark, and spoil their three grandchildren, Mason, Lyla, and Anya, who are already plotting their own adventures (and possibly a few museum exhibits of their own).

www.ingramcontent.com/pod-product-compliance
Lightning Source LLC
LaVergne TN
LVHW050324160826
845677LV00014B/3532
* 9 7 9 8 2 2 7 8 8 2 6 7 7 *